T0194133

SILENT, BUT SUPERHERO

RELEASING YOUR POWER AND PURPOSE

MINDSCOPE SEVEN

WESTBOW
PRESS®
A DIVISION OF THOMAS NELSON
& ZONDERVAN

WestBow Press books may be ordered through booksellers or by contacting:

WestBow Press
A Division of Thomas Nelson & Zondervan
1663 Liberty Drive
Bloomington, IN 47403
www.westbowpress.com
1 (866) 928-1240

Because of the dynamic nature of the Internet, any web addresses or
links contained in this book may have changed since publication and
may no longer be valid. The views expressed in this work are solely those
of the author and do not necessarily reflect the views of the publisher,
and the publisher hereby disclaims any responsibility for them.

Any people depicted in stock imagery provided by Getty Images are
models, and such images are being used for illustrative purposes only.
Certain stock imagery © Getty Images.

ISBN: 978-1-9736-2839-2 (sc)
ISBN: 978-1-9736-2840-8 (hc)
ISBN: 978-1-9736-2838-5 (e)

Library of Congress Control Number: 2018905583

Print information available on the last page.

WestBow Press rev. date: 05/29/2018

In loving memory of my mother. May your silence be honored and your voice ring out, through the lives you've touched both directly and indirectly.

CONTENTS

ACKNOWLEDGMENTS

Many thanks to my children. You have been a gift from heaven above. I'm eternally grateful for the privilege of being your mother. It allowed me to see love in its truest form—full of joy, sacrifice, difficulties, and triumphant victories. My words cannot fully express the blessing you both have been in my life—a life I would gladly trade for yours; a life that would have been empty without your presence.

Thanks also to my dear friend, TJP, who came into my life when I was in great need, and at my very worst. Your friendship demonstrated mercy, love, protection, and stability, allowing me a time for healing. Your friendship and care helped strengthen me, when I no longer believed I had the strength to survive. I thank God for sending you to my life.

A special thank-you to Dr. Angela Lauria. If not for the structure and steps of your program, I am certain that this manuscript wouldn't have been possible. I am blessed that God allowed our paths to intersect.

Another special thank-you to BF, for being the first person to offer meaningful perspective and assistance in a God-honoring way. I have much gratitude and respect for the help you offered through your understanding, and in setting me on a new path of love and acceptance of myself by denying the branded labels affixed to my soul.

Finally, I wish to acknowledge the following sources (listed alphabetically):

The Bible

Biblegateway.com

Biblehub.net

Biblestudytools.com

Cracked.com

http//departments.kings.edu

Desiringgod.org

GoodTherapy.org

Listverse.com

People-press.org

Pewresearch.org

Relevantmagazine.com

therichest.com, The Premium Network

www.smithsonianmag.com

Topteny.com

Wikipedia

But if the watchman see the sword come, and blow not the trumpet, and the people be not warned; if the sword come, and take [any] person from among them, he is taken away in his iniquity; but his blood will I require at the watchman's hand.

—Ezekiel 33:6 (KJV)

Meet Beatrix

My name is Beatrix. As a child, both the meaning of these two words—*integrity* and *authenticity*—and the harshness of a life in opposition to them, taught me lessons that I would carry throughout my life. It penetrated my soul, becoming both the pain of my existence and greatest gift. It carved and shaped me, just as a sculptor carves his stone. Initially this sounds harmless, but I grew to understand its curse. For the greater part of my life, I came to think of it as God's little joke on me, but I could not escape it clutches. I tried! I even argued with God, asking aloud, "Why? What were you thinking? Am I just your little sick joke to the world?" Of course, He never answered these questions grown from rebellion and usually voiced in a state of anger. Nevertheless, I stayed true to the course in my integrity, and tried my best to honor the standards of society without too much rebuttal. It seemed that I was always going against the grain. Even in my best attempts, I rubbed things and people in the wrong way. Still, I disciplined myself to its curse and suffering, no matter the sacrifice. Sure, I wanted to give up, and I often went into isolation, just to deal with the despair. While there, I would argue my points over in my head repeatedly, still coming to the same conclusion. I truly wanted to prove myself wrong and take the easier path. Oh, how I desired the easier path. But I had no choice because I understood the ugliness yielded from the alternative path. I had felt the sting of being on the wrong side of someone lacking integrity and authenticity. I understood the meaning of *underdog*. I just could never bear the thought of making another feel that type of pain. I could never bear the thought of acting or looking the way that I observed in others who did not maintain any sort of integrity or authenticity. I would hear their great words of honesty, observe their supposed authenticity and integrity, and then watch their actions display the exact opposite. Even as a child, I knew this was wrong. But because of this, I found it necessary to hide myself away. I could see that the numbers were greater on their side than mine. I knew there was no place for integrity, differences, or me. I had to stay under the radar and remain true to my design, but it made me feel like a fraud. Hypocritical people who were to teach me of trust and integrity made me an outsider. I knew there were only two choices: a path of loneliness and trying to sort things on my own, or a path of submitting to them and their terribly deceptive, mean-natured ways.

Even as a very young child, I had a clear understanding of the choices. I could either take the path of integrity, offering kindness, protection, and fair treatment to those in my path, and then accepting the position of outsider; or, I could take the broader path and submit to the will of those around me and perhaps even gain their love. My childhood brought me into a true consciousness of how my actions might impact others, especially the weak or vulnerable. I, too, was in the category of the weak, unwanted, and vulnerable, placed there by systems I was trapped within, in terms of both family and community. But I chose to always go the extra mile to protect or attempt to ease suffering of anyone I encountered on my path. I could always see the pain of another human. I wasn't trying to see it; I just could. I couldn't stand the thought of ignoring what I saw. I felt an overwhelming responsibility to ease the pain I recognized, since I was also one discarded and set aside, with few who cared or even noticed my existence. So, from a very early age, I decided to plug into the integrity of what was real and fight for those who could not fight for themselves. I chose to be alone, quietly refusing the false rewards of the unjust system I was thrust into. If I had to tolerate it for a period, it was only long enough to assess if I could indeed survive in that place with my integrity intact or stay just long enough to formulate my escape route. No one discussed the lesson of integrity, the cost of life with or without it. I learned its meaning through the actions of those around me, toward both me and others. When I would argue with myself about why I was doing this, weighing the cost of it into my present equation, I would hear the voice from God speak to my heart, reminding me of all the horrible outcomes resulting from traveling the easier and broader path. Still, I never understood this, because all my authority figures and most of society were doing the exact opposite—and it seemed they were getting ahead and enjoying life much more than I was. I would watch them, in wonder and confusion, thinking, *Why can't I do that? Just not care, throw caution to the wind. Just get what's mine.* That was what they were doing, with no problems, all benefits and happiness, it seemed. My frustration, anger, and isolation grew. I withdrew my true self even more. I knew there was no place in the sandbox of life for the likes of me. I began to internally refer to my situation as "My Blessing, and My Curse." I usually could make sense of everything after a bit of pondering; I would then sort it out and move on. But not this. How could something of such importance to basic truth of reality in our very existence be tossed around so flippantly?

The older I grew, the more disgusted I found it to be, because I could see the wake of its damages again and again. But still, no one else was alarmed or even really noticed it. It was accepted as the normal and even the popular thing to do. Where does one exist in a culture such as this? Was my thinking wrong? These were questions that, as I grew into adulthood, I had to answer for myself. I knew that without these answers, I might turn out like the very thing I abhorred so much. The years of watching and being its victim had left a permanent scar. Should I dip my toe in the water of less integrity and enjoy the advantages? I wished for the fun and carefree way of those around me. I wanted its perks and advancements, the same as others enjoyed. I had to make a choice. I made the choice of the more sacrificial path, not because I was a great person, but because I just didn't want to be ugly like the people I saw who traveled the broader path of deception. I chose to guide my life by integrity, by guarding my fellow humans from the very people who were choosing the other path containing only a frivolous pretend integrity. Nothing real.

I soon learned the difficulties of my decision. Choosing the rougher road of true integrity meant that I could take nothing for myself; instead, I found myself in the gap, always taking the heat for the well-being of others. This was the only meaningful thing that I drew from the well of integrity: helping me stay on its difficult and unrewarding path. I was in no way some angelic person; rather, the world viewed me more as a troublemaker or someone to keep an eye on. These are not good labels to receive. They immediately draw to the one labeled both dislike and mistrust from others. This is a big part of the reason why so many just toss integrity aside. Oh, everyone talks about how great integrity is, but we know its true reward. It becomes more of a luxury for the ones fortunate enough to land on the right side of the tracks. Allow me to explain. When you begin on the so-called wrong side of the tracks, many choices are based more on circumstances of urgency than the free space to think about the right or wrong of the matter. It becomes a sort of trigger response for self-protection. As a child, I watched the adults around me morph into new characters moment by moment. This did not escape me even then. I watched in frustration and questioned silently in my own mind, attempting to make sense of it. I clearly saw the disparity between what I heard being said one moment, and I observed being done the next. When the crowd changed, so did the words, opinions, and thoughts of the adult(s). I stood there, as a child, in complete confusion, nonetheless knowing I could not question it; I had best just keep my head down and my mouth shut. I studied it, though; oh, did I study it. I needed to make sense of it. I needed to understand it. I still remember how it made me feel. It was as if I were living in a parallel universe.

> I am tired and fed up with living my life according
> to the labels and boxes assigned to me by others!
> —Beatrix

CHAPTER 1

The Killing Begins

Beatrix as a Child

Beatrix and Fran were in the same class in elementary school. Their lives were in direct opposition, in every imaginable way. Beatrix was a highly aware child, most probably from environmental conditions, but perhaps by her very nature as well. As Beatrix told me stories of the happenings in her formative years, it was apparent just how early definitions begin in all our lives, and then how that begins translating and forming our future outcomes to some degree. There was a stark difference in the daily experiences of Beatrix and Fran, even at such young and tender ages. Let's take a glimpse into the home life of two children whose experiences were drastically different.

Each night, Fran got neatly and lovingly tucked into her bed, perhaps her parents even read her a bedtime story and gave her a good-night kiss. Maybe her parents told her of the exciting events to come the following day. The lights were shut off, and she felt the warmth of her loving parents and her cozy room. Whereas, a few streets away Beatrix—and others like her, both near and far away—experienced the fearful existence of a drunken, high, or violent parent (or parents) for the entirety of their days and nights. The homes of these children were riddled with holes in the walls, the property destroyed by the very people who should provide the safety, love, and stability necessary to form children's perception of trust. Their little minds were busy calculating how to be as quiet and invisible as possible to ensure one less argument or beating. Maybe they went to bed hungry, or had a sparing dinner divvied among them and their siblings to ensure that everyone was fed a small amount. No one ever tucked them in. They lay in their beds, frightened and stressed about what might happen that day or in the days to come. Their minds became overly active in the mode of survival of the war zone inside their own homes. They had nothing to look forward to the next day; every day was just another day to make it through and survive. This didn't even account for the safety and existence in the communities for each of these children.

So, with this simple example, we can ask, What are the differences in the state of mind for each child? Where does integrity even come into play when your every move is like a battlefield full of mines and traps that you must try to avoid in order to survive? With just this small glimpse at these very different environments, again, let's ask, How is integrity different for Fran and Beatrix (and other children like Beatrix)? One child has experienced healthy parenting and good examples of trust and integrity. The other's existence has shown that trust may result in sustaining harm, even at home.

Each of these children heads off to school, which becomes the first experience outside the home to reinforce the thoughts and beliefs, privilege or lack, for each child. Children naturally trust adults, not understanding, at such a young age, that much of their experiences have been tainted and even untruthful in many cases. The teacher has each of these two children—Fran and Beatrix—in the same classroom. One child becomes the apple of the teacher's eye; she can do no wrong. She comes running into the classroom each day, with a warm smile and lovely, clean clothes; she is vibrant, and ready for learning and fun. The teacher rewards these attributes with even more privileges for the child. Fran, and children like her, will most likely get put into the top-sector group in the classroom; they will be allowed more freedom and privileges in the classroom, and then they will begin wielding their designated power against easy targets: the children already beaten down by their home situations.

In sharp contrast, Beatrix, and children like her, come into the classroom tired, perhaps hungry, and begin reliving the tragedies from the night before. They continually worry about what will happen when they go back home that day. They worry all day long in the classroom about the threats awaiting them at home, planning for how they will respond and survive in their circumstances. They are carrying in a load of shame. Shame for feelings and events they do not understand. Shame for the clothing they wear, which other students have already pointed out. They are laughed at and mocked. The teacher often just turns a blind eye to all this; after all, these children don't matter anyway. They will never amount to anything. The teacher certainly does not want to have any beef with the in-crowd parents. It's easier to just look the other way. Meanwhile, children like Beatrix watch all this, and their growing minds once again value their self-worth to be, in a word, nothing. Again, all they feel is shame. Shame for not having money for lunch or at snack time. Shame for the messiness of their hair as they look around at the well-groomed children around them. They learn to either become very quiet or invisible, not wishing to be further embarrassed or targeted in the classroom. Or, they may morph into problem children, acting out in class in order to meet the standard of the label applied to them by trusted adults. The reaction exhibited usually depends on their personalities. In either case, these children are acting out under false pretenses, following the labels affixed to them and the categories, like neat little boxes, into which they have been conveniently placed.

I want a life no longer remiss to the actual
rooted problems and finally claim my own
truth and freedom!

—Beatrix

CHAPTER 2

The Thievery of Labels

Fast-Forward to Adult Beatrix

There she stood, weeping, gasping for air to calm herself. Her
exterior was strong. You could almost see the armor she wore.
Always stoic by nature, few knew her, and no one understood her,
although some claimed to. But I knew better; she would never
allow anyone to read or predict her feelings or thoughts. Beatrix,
forever calm in the storm, strong for everyone around her. She
had a way of making you feel so close to her, yet so far away. But
there she was, sobbing uncontrollably. I watched her gasping for
air, turning to face the wall as she desperately tried to gather her
herself. It was perplexing and saddening to watch. Beatrix became
a friend of mine. I was perhaps one of the few people she trusted,
but I even doubted that at times. But, somehow, I knew that I had
passed through gates that none had ever trod.

I had no idea how badly that day had affected her. She went quiet for
some time. I hadn't heard from her in sometime, but I figured she
just needed time. Finally, one day, she was on my voice mail once
again, sounding like herself. Wanting to stop by for a visit and to
catch up. I suspected something might be wrong. I knew that day,

the one when she broke down, wouldn't be glossed over as easily as she wanted it to appear. It uncovered more for Beatrix than even I could have imagined.

When I saw her, she looked different than I'd ever seen her. She looked deficient, even unhealthy, but she assured me that she was just tired and everything was fine. As we talked, she brought up that day. It was the day of her mother's passing. She told me the following account of that day, the day she walked in the room and first saw her mother after the accident. She explained how it felt like violent screaming inside her own mind: *"Silent no more!"* This was an anger that would not dissipate. She talked to no one in the room, as the anguish engulfed her.

Beatrix

How can this be happening? It wasn't supposed to happen this way. This is all wrong. These wounds that destroyed your body, are nothing compared to those you hold inside, invisible to others. They have no idea, Mama. I am so sorry. It wasn't supposed to end this way.

She was broken in what seemed to be a million pieces. Unrecognizable. This couldn't be happening.

Are you kidding me? Why did we do all this for so long? It wasn't supposed to end this way. You could have had peace, Mama; we all could have had peace. All our lives were given up and destroyed for what—this? Years of pretending and protecting one who cared for no one. The doctors came in then, interrupting my thoughts, and I still don't even know what they said. I placed my hand on hers and said, "Mama, this is Beatrix. I love you." Then, she gasped for air, her last breath. I knew she heard me, and then she was gone. She had taken her last breath. My chest grew tight and heavy; I couldn't catch my breath. They came in and took her body away and placed her in an adjacent room; they told us we could go in and spend time with her. I did; I had to look at her. I had to see what had happened to her. I slowly pulled back the covers, one section of her body at a time, and photographed what I saw. I needed to remember what I saw: the consequences of this life we lived. I spoke gently to her about my confusion. I knew her body couldn't hear me. But perhaps God would listen to my words and help me make sense of this tragedy. I wanted to pick her up from the table and take her home with me. I could visualize her waking up and pulling through, but I knew that image wasn't real. I stayed for a few more minutes, said my goodbyes, and left with the last most-tragic photographs of my mother. I kept repeating the same words over again in my head: *Silent no more, silent no more, silent no more. You don't have to be silent anymore, Mom. Never again! Your voice is just beginning to be heard.*

I made the commitment then and there, that very day, to never be silent again when someone was suffering or in trouble. I made the commitment to never be invisible again, to never be courteous to those who used, abused, and injured others.

Beatrix then spent some time explaining to me that she had always fought for people quietly. She explained that when she saw another in trouble, she would quietly go to work to shift the tide, stop unnoticed evil, and help protect the person who couldn't even see the oncoming train. She explained the importance of silence in dangerous situations. She understood how to shift the trajectory of a storm long before anyone else even knew it was there, and then divert it away from those in harm's way. With that, she smiled, but with the lick of fire in her eyes. This was a side of Beatrix she kept tucked away; few knew of this side of her. You could never imagine the fighter inside her, and that was exactly how she intended it to be.

She went on, explaining the many villainous plots she had overturned, with no one being the wiser. She laughed aloud; it delighted her. She found satisfaction in aiding and protecting those she felt were at risk. I would even say she felt responsible for doing so. She wasn't the type to look for these occasions, but if they crossed her path, she felt it was her duty to help those who could not help themselves. She felt that she would surely have to account for turning a blind eye to such horrible deeds done to another, or just standing by. This was never an option for Beatrix. I think part of it was because no one ever protected Beatrix; she had been alone for some time. She just couldn't watch someone hurt another, especially where there was an imbalance or misuse of power. She told me that she prayed for exactly the correct actions, according to her faith and for the situation she would encounter. I was so fascinated by the stories she told me. How could all of this be inside her? But it was. Beatrix, although stoic by nature, a real poker face, was also warmhearted, generous, and fiercely loyal to those she loved. This was the one line you should never cross with Beatrix. It was interesting how she accepted abuse from others but would never allow anyone to harm those she loved. She explained that she learned to enjoy watching the villainous ones when they discovered their plans had failed. She would revel in watching their tirades when they knew they were beaten, and yet had not a clue as to how.

Beatrix

When their despicable actions failed, and they were totally dumbfounded, I loved every moment of it. It was the only good I could find in such situations.

Beatrix told me of the anger she felt when watching those with power or authority, the ones we should be able to trust, using their power to abuse, deceive, harm, and even affect the ability of others to simply do their jobs. You know, the common working man or woman. The people who are struggling to get by, to raise their families, and then forced to watch the powerful take advantage of them.

Beatrix

You have but two choices: submit or fight. It's best to fight smart, quiet, and unnoticed. This is how you take space back, a little at a time, by staying under the radar and keeping conflict down. The optimal result is that no one gets hurt, and both parties benefit.

Beatrix told me of the times she heard coworkers and management laugh with one another about their disgusting acts against fellow employees and even customers. And then Beatrix talked more about her childhood, her mother, her siblings, and her father.

I wondered if I could have responded in the manner in which she had learned to operate. I wondered if had an ounce of the integrity that Beatrix had.

Beatrix

I decided that day, the day my mother died, to never be silent again when a person was in trouble, no matter what it meant for me. I made myself a promise to never be silent again, because I understood the ending. The Wednesday before my mother's death, my gut told me to go and check on mom, but I didn't go. I didn't go because I knew it would be like every other time when I went there; it would take me days to recover, so, I didn't go. Could I have changed what happened? I've asked myself this question so many times. I will never make that mistake again! Why do the people we love so much rarely love us in return? I have never been able to answer this question.

Beatrix explained that she had played out the ending of the lives of her mother and siblings many times before. It had been a happy ending, but the ending for her mother wasn't happy at all; it was tragic. It was disgusting.

Beatrix told me, "There is no other choice now that I understand this." Her entire life had come into sharp focus; it was defined that day.

Beatrix

If I could ask my mother now, "Mom, if you knew then what you know now, what would you have told me? What would you have told all of us? Would our lives have turned out differently?"

And then Beatrix explained that she knew she was responsible for changing this for her own children. She wanted them to have the life she never had—to have freedom, happiness, and love, and to be free from "all of this mess," as she put it.

Beatrix

I know that the way and time in which my mother passed is just one of the messages that God has for me.

Her mother's death was a violently painful exit. Beatrix—a loving woman, a sacrificing woman, a good woman, a woman of greater integrity and authenticity than I have ever known—told me this in response to her mother's death: "I took that vow to never be silent again when witnessing the abuse of another. And I meant it. No matter the cost—never again."

CHAPTER 3

Drug Dealers Meet the "Killed" and the "Thieved"

This is where we begin to understand the consequences and drug of choice for those who experienced circumstances similar to those of Beatrix and her family. We can see how their ability to survive and cope daily became a situation riddled with danger and offering few options. This is what they endured in their day-to-day lives as the result of an abuse of power: they were labeled as a means of control, confined to exist in boxes designed by others. It changed everything about their lives in ways more complicated than we can even imagine. After spending much time with Beatrix, I knew her story would help others who might need guidance or perspective in overcoming the circumstances of their lives—lives stolen from them right before our eyes. Through the advantage of a fast-forwarded time frame, we can examine the outcomes of such paths, and thereby allow opportunity for adjustment. We will be able to see the great depths and roots of the problems, and how, as these roots grow, they reach like tentacles to places never imagined, eventually choking out life from all in their grasp.

So, I asked Beatrix to share her story, and we will discover her story together as I provide guidance in understanding the root causes and their effects, and then devising solutions to overcome them. Her story will inspire you to see life in a whole new way, by viewing the problems and seeing how Beatrix masterfully and mindfully fought to surmount them. Beatrix explained to me that she came to realize the difficulties she faced were only a God-given path of discovery and growth. She told me that she now understands the connection between our own individual circumstances and those of others, and how this connection could also offer the assistance needed to solve many problems in the world today.

> We are to give back all that we receive. It's our singular most important purpose while on this earth: to live the life God had in mind upon our creation, by denying all other power, opinion, and influence as falsehoods.
>
> —Beatrix

"The Hostages"

As children, we are all assigned roles, positions, and values based on the systems we are born into, including family, gender, race, religion, and culture. For many, this is a positive, even a privilege. For others, it becomes a place of certain opposition, persecution, and confinement to minimal opportunities. Their lives begin behind the eight ball, where there are two choices: fighting to overcome or accepting to succumb. When people are confined to the walls built by another, they are painfully aware of the consequence of any escape attempt. They become so lodged into their perspective corners that a mere wiggle can set off a wave of events that make their lives even more burdensome. Do they dare even think about freedom? Is there anyone on the other side who might see them, or have they now become totally invisible? The foregoing reflects a system of ideas and values designed by those in authority and then widely accepted by the masses. Any attempt to question the status quo either makes one appear to be a troublemaker or an individual in need of stricter confinement. You ponder every possible means for escape. You watch the others around you, laughing and enjoying the lightheartedness of their very different world that holds possibilities and a future of hope.

As we grow from children to teenagers, we attempt to make shifts within our enclosed quarters. Our anguish grows, and our anger rises; but we are still young, and we tell ourselves great tales of what our futures might be like. Those of us who have grown increasingly angry begin to rebel against the life defined by the ones who captured our souls in childhood. As a result of that anger, some of us find a new family, on the streets, where our boundaries widen, leading us to feel envious of what we see, causing us to devise ways in which to take our revenge against a society that isolated us to a land of poverty, crime, and homelessness, where we then grew increasingly ill minded with an ever-increasing and contagious madness that swallowed us whole. Others of us, while still recognizing the anger, began to believe that we could rise above and be better. If we gave those in power the chance to see just a hint of our true selves, perhaps they would allow us to step into their world, even if merely to act as their servants. Perhaps this would be our way out, our way to a better life, where our children might have greater opportunities than we had.

Here we are now, in our adult form. How can this be happening? Everything is falling apart right before our eyes. As we look around, it seems people are dazed and confused. Do you ever find yourself wondering, *Can this really be happening? Did anyone just see that? What's going on here?* And then you begin to debrief your own thoughts, afraid to say anything out loud, for you no longer understand the rules or logic in society. No, you are not crazy. If you find yourself thinking this, don't panic! You're probably a forward thinker who can quickly grasp the landscape and what comes next. You may even be an innovative thinker and problem solver looking toward the future. However, a greater number of individuals in society can't see things quite that immediately. That's one of the reasons you, and those of us like you, find ourselves in this quagmire. The good news is that everyone can learn these skills. We have reached the boiling point in society, and collectively we must begin to find solutions. We are losing the battle in society at every level. Parents face near-impossible hurdles daily in terms of keeping their children safe and stable. We are a war-torn society, riddled with poverty, overspending, addiction, abuse, terrorism, racism, and many more evils. You name it, and we are fighting about it. Across the world, we have lost regard and respect for most every entity that previously helped stabilize our families and communities. This leaves us in a most confusing predicament, and we see the results of that frustration each day on the news. We will discover the roots of what ails us and the soothing balms we so desperately need. We must find new approaches that will guide us safely through this transitional period. If you have interest in learning to decipher, decode, negotiate, and maneuver in today's ever-changing landscape, you will not be empty-handed when you finish reading this book. Clearly, we need new tools to face and move into the future. The great news is that if we can successfully meet and greet the necessary changes, we can create a society that functions more effectively for one and all.

Where Are We Now?

Blue-Collar Workers, Small-Business Owners, Families

These individuals are frustrated with society around them. They have been the backbone of society, working for average salaries, living somewhat dull but responsible lives, and now they look around and feel cheated. They are largely underrepresented and invisible slaves for society, as they are the largest working group of society. Many of them have lost their jobs at companies where they worked loyally, and they find themselves in the black hole of no assistance when they are down. Many of them are small business owners who feel a growing despair as more regulations and tax burdens are placed on their businesses. These individuals, whether workers or small-scale owners, grew up in the time when the integrity of a person's word was everything. They lived it, worked it, and breathed it, only to find it all for naught. They now find themselves in a society that they feel has bled them dry for those whom they view as lazy undesirables. They feel forgotten and discarded, primarily the ones who built the foundations of society. They see no place for them in an ever-changing society. Their lives have been greatly affected by the shift, and they aren't equipped to navigate the changes. They feel ripped off. They know they worked diligently and behaved responsibly, and this irks and hurts them as they stand amid brokenness and despair. Their jobs are being targeted and given to less-qualified or less-serious workers, as companies have taken on a new model built for cheap, turnover labor. These individuals see this as just the beginning of their troubles. Many find themselves unemployed and without health insurance, their families broken and full of despair, and this often leads to the thralls of addiction. They are worried about their children navigating the dangerous and confusing world, with no integrity or morals to guide them. Their children brush them off as ignorant or too old school for them. Their children are lost and confused by the facade of society. Most in this group grew up very independent of parenting, but their children suffer from overparenting. This has created a total divide, leaving little room for the youth to respect their elders at all. The older adults lived in a time of the economic rise, many remembering a time of having little. This created a more appreciative mind-set and a different type of work ethic. They started on the bottom rung, and only by hard

the balance of labor to their value. They expect top-level positions, right out of the gate, feeling that if they can't get the prestige, money, attention, and recognition they believe they deserve, they will opt out completely, making themselves dependent on their parents and society. They prefer leisure to work—and view these leisure pursuits as part of what they are entitled to—and they spend most of their time hanging out with friends, using drugs, and consuming alcohol in the extreme, and represent one of the most liberal sexualized generations that we have seen in years. The internet and social media have also impacted the thoughts of this generation, especially around sexuality. They are exposed to mature subjects while their minds are still very immature. This creates a sense of normalcy as to sexually deviant thinking and behavior. Even if their parents attempted to limit this type of exposure, there was always a kid at school to provide the unwanted exposure. This group has taken on the idea of us against them (adults), although they have provided little to nothing to a society that they enjoy living in; after all, to them, life is a party. Many of them are moving back in with their parents or never leaving the household. They show very little respect or regard for the parents who gave them the privilege and opportunity they have enjoyed. Now society must face the task of getting them trained for a rapidly changing world. It is imperative for them to gain an understanding of how to navigate the landscape that is much different from any that we have ever known. Our youth will be ill prepared to face the world as it continues to evolve, especially when they face peers who weren't as privileged but were prepared better for the future of our world. What will this discrepancy mean for our youth, if we can't begin to close this gap of preparedness and grasping the future? We must not leave these doors open for much longer, or these young people will find themselves dumbfounded, in shock, and at the mercy of unknowns.

White-Collar Workers, Leaders
and Management, Families

This group will be at greater risk if tensions continue unchecked in society and the world. They will find themselves greatly outnumbered, at risk, and ill equipped when the paradigm shifts. The average person in this demographic is detached from the reality of mainstream society, uninformed, and out of touch with the basic realities of society at large. This is mostly to the result living in a bubble, as they rarely cross over to interact in a meaningful way in the very lives of those who work for them, serve them, or inhabit the greater space of society. This has led to great misunderstandings between them and the average human. Because of this, mistrust has grown, drawing even deeper lines of division. The people of this demographic have kept a distance for a variety of reasons: some perhaps justified; others completely mythical. The objective for this demographic is to gain a real understanding of the patterns formed over time that have caused this great divide, which is now causing the underserved to grow restless and dangerous. The group of fortunate must not allow themselves to revert to past thinking or ideas, because the landscape has changed. Throughout history, they have held little consequence or responsibility for the unjustified discriminations delivered to most of humankind. They need training and assistance in mediating the damaging differences between them and the greater part of society. The training and mediations should be provided by a source that can provide a fair approach and be dedicated to removing labels from both sides and adjusting the thoughts and approach that created the negatives. By and large, the old recurring problems in society have been met with ineffective and costly solutions that have backfired on all sides of socioeconomic status. This has created a system of dependence, furthered confusions, and resulted in the landscape in which we now reside: a toxic land field of labeled people, ill-minded thoughts, and failed approaches, all of which is quickly spinning out of control. This group must begin to adjust their thoughts in a sincere way, and then combine it with appropriate actions to lessen the divide. This most definitely should be a fair approach for all parties, understanding that those who are currently taking advantage must also undergo changes as well. By creating a fair and balanced existence for all of humankind, it lessens the burden and frustration for all parties. As we have seen, this has not been successfully done by government or politicians, on account of conflicts of interest for both. This is a ground-level problem, and the solutions can only be devised and provided by humankind itself, with all people making the sacrifices and changes needed.

Emergency Workers, Law Enforcement, Prison Systems, Government Agencies, Community Organizations

As tensions and danger grows around the world, the individuals in this group must deal with more than they can handle, given the current training and tools in place. It is necessary for them to build bridges in the communities they serve in order to maintain peace and regain understanding, trust, and order. The current us-against-them mentality it will only brew a much more dangerous culture. They have been more reliant on building relationships with the lawbreakers and have left the greater asset of average law-abiding citizens out of the loop. The more they can train and *authentically* team up with the citizens, the greater the number of relationships they will build, which in turn will be very instrumental in shifting the power and authority back to where it should be: with law enforcement and law-abiding citizens. This will also mean that these departments will have to look within and extract any corruptness from the inside by retraining where necessary. If they continue to deal within their corrupt systems, they are sure to become overwhelmed and find their jobs to be increasingly difficult. This group is also dealing with negative labels applied to them, which makes their jobs increasingly difficult and miserable. This can be adjusted by teaming up with the citizens in meaningful ways and building tight relationships of trust and commitment.

Our eyes are open now. There is no "true" bubble of segregation. Any attempt of drawing this line of division always comes to a cataclysmic end for everyone. We are all feeling the temperature rise, but we are not quite sure what to do or even where to begin. We are all aware of the pressing need for new tools to help us deal with the complex and dangerous problems all around us. We need improved ability to accurately read the landscape. The current labeling system of society has exhausted its stay, created toxic thinking, and thereby led us down a disastrous path. We have an opportunity to retrain our minds and develop new approaches to lead us into the future. The snapshots of a variety of demographic groups afford us a view from different perspectives than our own. We all hold part of the truth and part of the responsibility for the current problems. Unless we successfully unite, learning from our mistakes and respecting our differences, the violence and disasters will continue and increase. This storm that humanity has brewed can also be the turning point of transition.

We all are feeling the effects, realizing the past attempts haven't succeeded. With the growing frustration, if we are not careful, we may take incorrect approaches, negating the opportunity within our grasp. By now, we have all been so programed to believe falsehoods that we think we can only discuss things that make people feel happy and comfortable. We have become a society preferring to live altered versions of reality, ensuring the comfort needed to maintain the complacency. We become angry if someone truthfully speaks reality as it actually is. We don't want to hear about responsibility for our own fair share of the mess, much less what must be done for to achieve the cleanup. We have become so accustomed to this lifestyle that it becomes almost impossible to view the devastating shifts in society that are right before our eyes. We do our best to wall it off, even though it has reached our doorsteps.

Collectively, we hold the answers for our own resolve. Combining our knowledge and efforts successfully and peacefully will allow us to actively reclaim our families, communities, and world. The storm we see is just the beginning and should be revered as a warning signal. We must seize this window of opportunity to create the change so desperately needed. Our response will dictate our outcome: the future world in which our children will be left to survive. We mustn't continue the state of complacency and repeated mistakes. If this continues, our future will be one of looking back at the rubble, regretting missed opportunity. So, how do we begin, and where to we place our energy and resources first?

We begin by acknowledging the warning signals going off, and then refusing dishonest narratives set out to stop progression. To successfully transition through a major paradigm shift requires removing labels of definition from the past, and then openly learning the truth of one another. Only through honesty in both approach and intent will we experience gainful new change.

For each person, living a life that isn't who they each know themselves to be or be capable of will manifest itself differently, largely based upon individual personalities and/or the labeled positions held in the family or atmosphere. For instance, Beatrix was viewed as the unwanted daughter, whereas her sister, Anna, was the apple of her mother's and father's eye. This wasn't the fault of Anna as a child; she, too, was labeled, and she had to live out that label or suffer consequences. However, the label for Beatrix wasn't exclusive to the home environment. Her parents carried the designed message of control to the outward community, even creating falsehoods. Beatrix had no desire to hurt anyone, not even her parents. She always held on to hope that healing would come to her family, and then understanding and restoration. That isn't what happened, as we have seen, at least up to this point.

Beatrix knew in her heart what she had to do. What she finally had to gain the courage to do, no matter how difficult, painful, or scary. She knew she had a fight. She understood what she was up against. She made up her mind after her mother's passing, that even death would be better than the life she had led up to that point. A life that wasn't her own. A life dictated and designed by her father, mother, and spouse. She was lost and invisible in the midst of their selfish games of control, manipulation, and trickery. She couldn't allow this toxic wasteland to take a toll on her, or her children, any longer. She wanted them to have a chance at freedom and lives of their own. Not that of a cultish, controlling nature that eventually breaks every human in its path, either to submission or defeat. She decided this would not be the fate of her own children, and her ending would not be likened to her mother's. She understood the end results of the madness and decided she would be strong enough for the change needed, even if it were her own demise.

She discovered, in her difficult journey, that this wasn't just her fight. God had led her out because He knew what she did not. He was leading Beatrix on a journey of faith that turned out to be one she could hardly believe. A journey that led her to a war—a war fought for all those suffering in hidden, dark, and silent places. Beatrix was in for the fight of her life, and she knew it. But this time, she would fight! She would stand until her death, if need be. As she described the amazing journey with God, I was left astonished. I couldn't believe her story, but it was real. It was real and authentic, just as Beatrix herself was. Perhaps this was why God used Beatrix as such an instrument. He knew exactly what she would do and how she would respond. Beatrix explained to me, always in tears of gratitude, what she had discovered. "I conquered the impossible. I should not even be alive to tell this story, but I am!" She declared to me more times than I can recount, "God can be trusted. I want everyone to know and understand this!"

Beatrix: Toxic Effects of Life as a Hostage

It was as if I had just enough time to catch my breath before being shoved back under the water again, fighting for a gasp of air, hoping to escape. I would see their faces at the surface of the water above me, laughing at me as I surfaced to the top to take a breath. The three of them, laughing aloud and shoving me back under the water again. This was exactly what their treatment felt like—slowly drowning.

But I was hopeful, ever trying to please, always thinking, *It's okay.* I was the I-will-fix-it-for-everyone machine. That was what I had become. Well, partly I had to be, and then, partly I had grown to believe I was supposed to do this. I was lower than they were. They made me believe it, and over time, I believed it more and more. I was surrounded by fear, torment, and confusion ever since I was a child. I learned to survive, do whatever it took to make it stop. Perhaps this sink-or-swim environment made me a fighter; I don't really know.

How can any of this be happening? I find myself lost in a sea of raging confusion, fear, anger, and doubt, with no idea which fire to extinguish first. I need to think, to concentrate. *Oh goodness, I can't even think anymore. What's happening? How did I get here? How did we all get here?* I thought I could hold it all together; after all, I have worked so diligently at doing exactly what I was supposed to do. My thoughts raced back and forth. *Not today! Not on my watch! Not ever again!* But, deep down, I'd always known this day would come.

The final straw breaking the camel's back. I always knew, even as a scared little girl, that a showdown between my father and me would happen. I would get the courage to break free from his sick, mean control system. I imagined it in so many ways, each one a little different. But I never imagined it would be like this. I thought the damage would be more isolated, that I would be able to handle it like every time before. I had grown accustomed to mistreatment, never fitting in, always being misjudged, to the point of accepting this as normalcy for my life. After a while, you numb yourself to the pain, you turn your head to the underhanded actions meant to obstruct whatever you attempt. You still quietly hope for change, even ignoring the injustices and mistreatments, making excuses for them. But this time it's different. The words still echo in my head: "Silent no more!" I can no longer ignore it. Living in toxic wastelands of abuse or oppression holds no hope. You try to tell yourself it's possible, but it's not. I still have a chance to take my life back. I am still alive. I still have a chance to aid my children in a better future. If not, how can I live with myself, with what I know? I have seen how it ends in tragedy. I can't allow myself or my children to absorb, or inherit, any more of this. God reassured me: "Be still. Be silent. Do nothing. Let them show you who they are and believe them!" That is exactly how it began, and exactly what I did. He commanded my silence and told me not to lose my authenticity—because someone needed to see it. I had no idea what this meant; however, I knew that it was very serious, fraught with danger. I knew I would be alone again, with only God to rely upon. It was the most terrifying prospect of my life. I figured it would be my end, but, even so, I still walk willingly and carefully in His will.

So many families are like the family of Beatrix. By growing up in a system of intolerance for her unique characteristics, and in a family of limited acceptance, she simply did not meet any of the standards desired of her. She did her best to blend in, and yet still maintain the integrity of authentic self. This made fitting into the mold increasingly difficult. She could no longer accept a placement of design by those who never offered her love or support, but, rather, further ostracization. It became a now-or-never situation for Beatrix. She knew her life was fleeting.

Command them to do good, to be rich in
good deeds, and to be generous and willing to
share. In this way they will lay up treasure for
themselves as a firm foundation for the coming
age, so that they may take hold of the life that
is truly life.

—1 Timothy 6:18–19 (NIV)

CHAPTER 4

Superhero Rules

Foundational Truth

Any well-executed plan has a set of foundational rules to keep the
troops both safe and on task. In the heat of battle, humans will
automatically revert to the lesser of emotional responses, which
creates devastating consequences. To ensure the proper execution
of a mission, you must limit human-judgment errors and mistakes.

In our daily life, we plan well for our jobs, in hopes of advancement
and for fear of reprimand. Most of us would never consider being
haphazard at our jobs because we understand that our basic
survival relies on our performance level. We spend almost as
much time planning social events with our friends or communities.
But, somehow, our minds seem to grow complacent on the more
important things, such as our own personal development and the
well-being of our family. For most, it's not a conscious effort of
disregarding the more important things; instead, complacency
eases in on us unexpectedly. So, when we are already stressed

and overly busy, how do we direct our attention and efforts to the things that are most important? The good news is that the solution will not take any additional time. It will be a few adjustments of your current time and efforts. But, more importantly, it will require your attentiveness through a conscious mind. Most of us aren't geared to having a superconscious state of mind, because thinking is difficult. Instead, we settle for going through the motions, just going with the flow of life, society, or those around us.

When I discuss developing oneself, I am not speaking of the outer ego self, but, instead, the inner world where our conscience resides, and is either actively working to help us in decision-making, or just lying dormant. By adulthood, most of us have nearly detached completely from the inner world and begin to rely on exterior manipulations to be our source for guidance and decisions. Unfortunately, we see more people living out a life of detachment in today's world. This didn't happen to us overnight. It was a slow progression over time, and now we find ourselves in this confusing state of frustration. Our judgment is tested throughout each day, making it imperative to have a system in place to guide us through the most routine tasks and the most critical planning.

So, what ensures our success at making the best judgment in each situation? Is it our intelligence, religion, and cultural influence, or is it just self-fulfillment that directs our thoughts, decisions, and actions daily? Most never question their own judgment, and they have no litmus test in place that is free from outer conflicts of interest. Most operate more on autopilot mode, usually with emotions and ego as the guide. Can you pinpoint a time when emotions or ego led you to incorrect or even self-destructive choices? Of course, even the most conscientious person has been guilty of this catastrophic process more than once. In such instances, I am sure you found yourself with less-than-desirable outcomes, wishing that you could turn back the hands of time. None of us can go backwards in time; however, we can learn valuable new processes from mistakes. We must create a guide for ourselves in which we can take ownership of the choices we make and the whys behind them, and then muster the stamina to use this guide to see us through to our desired destination. A well-developed set of foundational rules should be a set of truths bigger than our own selfish desires and egos. This should be an unexplainable power that is bigger, stronger, and smarter than we are. Many refer to this as faith in a Higher Power; for me, this is God. It took many years for me to understand faith beyond its mere definition as a word. I mean an understanding of how to actively live life in a state of faith. This may sound crazy, even ridiculous, when there is no guide in place, no real tangible proof of power above all, our proverbial trump card, so to speak, for all matters. Gaining access to the power of the Alpha and Omega at our disposal requires our walking in faith through the fiery trials before us.

Beatrix on Faith

I attempted to do this for many years, and I just couldn't make the pieces of puzzle fit into any recognizable solution to anything. Maybe it was immaturity, or lack of wisdom or experience. Whatever the case, once I made this discovery, everything changed. I don't mean in a frivolous way; instead, it was nothing less than miraculous. I felt afraid to even claim it at times, fearing that people might say I was being dishonest or even crazy. And that did happen.

When you make a discovery, you know how excited you are and how you just have a need to tell someone? Then, when you do, it's the biggest letdown because they don't believe it, and you begin to feel bad about telling them. And then you may even question the reality yourself. The entire point of faith is the belief in what cannot be proved. But without faith, without a force bigger than yourself, you are left to depend on the whims of uncertainty, what's popular at the time, or the random opinions of others. The foundational rules you establish for yourself will be the root of everything you choose for your future self. We face many choices each day, running the gamut of importance, from whether we will participate in the office-cooler gossip, to what we should do about a significant relationship. Trust me; I know this, having tried numerous ways of resolve as I was maturing. However, my most-miraculous, life-changing moments came from standing in the unknown place of faith. It came from a place of brokenness, where I knew for certain that life and the people around me could not be relied upon or trusted. This is a most important point, because when the stakes got higher than I could afford, it forced me to rely completely on a Higher Power. I pushed all my chips in and struck a deal. I realized most of my life had been given to those who weren't willing, or weren't even capable of, being my friend, much less anything beyond that. A most bitter pill to swallow. My life felt like a failure, as if my choice of a life of integrity and sacrifice had let me down. What was the meaning of any of it? I was furious with myself for being so stupid, yet I still did not buy into the alternative. So, now what? In my calculation, it would either be the end or the beginning; but, no matter what, I had to break free from the labels and boxes keeping me confined and living a life as others dictated, rather than as God had purposed and designed me for. It wasn't going to be easy, and there was much at stake—much to lose. In a moment of deep desperation, I heard the voice of God speak a single truth to me. He continued to repeat the same words as I prayed, looking for other answers. His words to me were "Let them show you who they are; be still, be silent, do nothing, and believe them this time." These words became the critical turning point for my life. As I began this journey, I had to keep repeating this to myself in order to stay strong. I knew that I would need some tools for my journey. The first one of these being a truth so substantial that it would be rendered unbreakable in the storms I needed to pass through. The most difficult times to walk in faith are those when the storm is tossing you in every direction, and you see no end in sight. This first tool, *truth,* that I placed in my belt for the journey became the most important foundation of support as I walked into the darkness of the abyss, having no idea if I would make it out. I was alone, but I had always been alone, just not willing to accept the reality.

Truth will be your strength for all that lies ahead. When confusion and weariness surround you, it is imperative to have truth as a rock to steady you. Your humanness will cause you to question in the heat of battle, and without truth, you will stray from safety. Also, remember that you will be adjusting your foundational rules as you grow and develop into a more mature version of yourself. As you are developing your personal reference, try to rid yourself of societal rules, although some of society's views may happen to coincide with your own. Just don't use society as a guide or foundation because it is not truth, and is ever changing with time. Truth does not change. It stands the course of time, and it is reliable. Our understanding of truth may change, but the truth never actually changes. As our understanding grows, so does our wisdom, our deeper truth of self and then of optimal choices.

A Look Back in Time

> Multiplying life through redemption of time; time heeds no man!
>
> —MindScope Seven

The "theories" for the causes listed below are drawn from what various historians have suggested. They are called theories because they are based on reasonable information (or were, when they were first proposed) and make some sense in explaining the phenomena. Each theory below describes the main idea briefly. These are but a few historical atrocities acted out by humans against other humans, driven by fear, deception, hate, greed, complacency, pride, and dreadful ignorance (both actual and accepted).

Each day, we are faced with decisions about how and what to allocate our time toward. Will it be work, social events, our families, our faith, or nothing at all? We take time for granted, as if it's never ending. I want you to reflect on the snapshots of "Where we are now," from an earlier chapter, in contrast to some historical events shared in this chapter. As you read and think about the use of time, both now and in history, ask yourself what time may be offering us presently. By holding present-day time and historical time up in the light of contrast, what might the view teach us that is of critical importance today? How can understanding the tragedy from the past help us make different decisions to change our future? Could it be an opportunity for us to make different choices to help alter our future and the future of our children? Could it offer a fast-forward look, like that experienced by Beatrix at her mother's passing? If you remember, she could clearly see the ending, and it changed her life that day. The decisions she would make, and the fights she would take on for herself and others, completely changed that day.

More frequently than we like to acknowledge, humankind has shown the propensity to use time inappropriately, ignoring despicable acts against humanity. Can we learn from our mistakes? Can we gain the courage to look at the reality surrounding us before it's too late, once again? Let's look at just a few tragedies in history, when humans lost their way, acting upon hatred, greed, unrealistic fears, misinformation, and a host of wrong thinking. We all look back and ask ourselves, "How could that have ever happened?" But, are we in a similar position now? Could we be headed toward a mass extinction of humankind, of our own doing? We have only two choices of what we do with time: (1) take proactive steps to alter the trajectory of our destination beforehand; or, (2) stand in disillusionment in the aftermath, wondering how we ever allowed this outcome to occur.

Cambodian Genocide: 2.5 Million Dead

Pol Pot, also known as Hitler of Cambodia, attempted to recall the agrarian socialist agenda in order to revive the country's days of glory. Pol Pot sought to create a utopia with his regime's categories of ethnicity and religion, turning a blind eye to foreign aid. Cambodia's minorities, such as Vietnamese, Chinese, Muslims, Christians, and Buddhists, encountered mass execution, displacement, and hard labor, from the mid-1970s to nearly the end of that decade. Around twenty thousand mass grave sites in Cambodia, called killing fields, are considered as an evidence of the severe and intolerable acts carried out by Pol Pot's communist Khmer Rouge system. By 1979, 25 percent of the Cambodian population had been exterminated.

Nigerian Civil War: 3 Million Dead

For Nigeria, the story begins with independence from Britain in 1960. The three biggest ethnic groups—the Igbo, Hausa, and Yoruba—started struggling for political power in the country. By 1966, a series of messy coups and countercoups by the Muslim Hausas in the north began executing the region's Christian Igbos. The Igbos fled to the southeast and attempted secession from Nigeria. Only five countries in the world officially recognized their new independent Republic of Biafra.

The Nigerian government launched an assault. Within a year, it captured Biafra's oil fields and virtually all its revenue sources. By the end of 1967, Biafra's food supplies were cut. Within months, 50 percent of Igbos lay starving in their new republic, while hundreds of thousands more were brutally slaughtered by the Nigerian army. By the time Biafra surrendered in 1970, three million Igbos had been murdered.

Slave Trade: Estimated 2 to 5 Million Dead

Historian Manisha Sinha from the University of Massachusetts has estimated that two million to five million might have perished in the Atlantic slave trade, which included slaves bound for South America, the Caribbean, and North America. (Other historians have focused exclusively on the North American slave trade.)

So, what's the American share? Starting in the late 1960s, historians began culling hard numbers on the slave trade, using shipping manifests and other original documents. The result is the Trans-Atlantic Slave Database. It has tabulated an estimated 80 percent of the traffic in human beings and found that about 10.7 million people survived the passage from their homelands, between 1500 and 1866. Of that number, about 390,000 made it to North American soil (approximately 3 percent of the total).

Much data is missing, either because it was lost or because no records were kept of the illegal shipments of slaves to North America that took place after 1808. That was the year when the United States banned the importation of slaves from Africa. The database counts only the deaths resulting from the capture and transport of slaves; it does not include the people who died in bondage from brutality, disease, and/or deprivation.

Holodomor: 7.5 Million Dead

Ukrainian for *hunger-extermination*—caused by the Soviet Union from 1932 to 1933—this was Stalin's artificially engineered famine to cause the genocide of the Ukrainian people.

In the late 1920s, Stalin's collectivized agriculture coerced Ukrainian farmers to give up their private land and property and, instead, to work state-owned factory farms. The aim wasn't specifically to feed Soviet cities, but, rather, to provide surplus exports to make the state enough money to meet Stalin's ambitious industrial targets. When the majority of Ukrainian farmers resisted, Stalin launched class warfare.

Soviet troops confiscated Ukrainian land, livestock, and property en masse. Families were evicted, crammed into freight trains, and shipped to Siberia, without food or shelter, and left there to perish. But the final "crushing blow" (Stalin's words) was the impossible increases in Ukraine's agricultural quotas, which the territory was of course unable to meet. The Soviet government then decreed harsh policing and raids across the territory, confiscating food supplies and tightening the belt of the already-starving Ukraine. In mid-1933, famine killed thirty thousand people a day. Stalin denied any starvation was occurring, and exported millions of tons of grain.

In 2008, European Parliament officially recognized the Holodomor as a premeditated crime against humanity. Holodomor Memorial Day is now commemorated in Ukraine, on the fourth Sunday of every November.

Holocaust: 17 Million Dead

Easily the most well-documented genocide in history, the Holocaust was Nazi Germany's systematic violence against Jews. The Holocaust exterminated approximately two-thirds of all Jews living in Europe (from 1933 to 1945), with a sheer scale of systemic capture, enslavement, and execution made possible by a network of more than forty thousand death facilities fed by brutal anti-Semitic legislation and nationalist propaganda throughout the German Third Reich of World War II. But the six million murdered Jews weren't the only victims of Hitler's Aryan utopia.

The 1935 Nuremberg Laws—which legally removed basic rights and work freedoms for Jews—were expanded on November 26, 1935, to include Romanians, blacks, traveling people, and all their offspring as "enemies of the race-based state": the same category given to Jews. Many slowly starved, many labored in slavery until death, and many simply disappeared. But the most horrible images that remain are the factory-like death camps, where prisoners were marched like cattle into mechanized slaughterhouses designed to poison, burn, and dispose of hordes of human beings, with utmost efficiency. For more details about The Nuremberg Laws: https://www.archives.gov/publications/prologue/2010/winter/nuremberg.html

Mass Rape in Germany

By the end of World War II, Berlin had fallen into the hands of the Soviets and been left in ruins. Germany faced multiple troops occupying the country, with widespread looting and mass rape. Reportedly, the Soviet Army was blamed for the rape of up to 2 million women and children, as well as the murder of as many as 240,000 civilians. Unfortunately, this is believed to be the biggest mass rape in history. Surprisingly, the large-scale rape was not only the Soviets' responsibility; the Americans and the French were accused of mass rape as well, yet on a smaller scale.

European Colonization of the Americas: Up to 100 Million Dead

A handful of reasons make this a disputed entry as the biggest genocide in recorded history, but if you believe that the collective disregard of one ethnic group's basic human rights (or more than one group, for that matter), or that the normalized practice of subverting the way of life of an entire population, can be called crimes against humanity, then you probably won't take issue with condemning the near extinction of North American indigenous peoples by European colonialism.

The genocide question here remains complex. For one, human rights, as we know them today, didn't exist for much of the time of Europe's colonial expansion, and the very term *genocide* didn't arise until the twentieth century. But Columbus's so-called discovery of the Americas, in 1492, initiated an explosion in European wealth and power, which ended in Europe's total control of the Western Hemisphere by the twentieth century, and the death of 95 percent of American indigenous peoples.

Hence, the colonization of the Americas denotes not a single act of killing, but, rather, a long phenomenon of displacement, disease, and subjugation of previously thriving native populations. In many respects, conflict and violence were mainstays of conquest, and European colonists, by definition, worked to displace indigenous groups. But the lines of premeditated genocide start blurring when the simple fact of European contact, and the resultant introduction of European diseases, caused the overwhelming majority of indigenous deaths. To be sure, European settlers did very little to mitigate their catastrophic impact on the aboriginal way of life.

The Pontic Genocide: Estimated 450,000 to 750,000 Dead

As victims of one of the most brutal war crimes, the Pontian Greeks spent nine years surrounded by the death and destruction of innocent lives. For racist and religious reasons, the Ottoman Empire perpetrated violence against the poor and different ethnic and religious groups, erroneously believing that they, the Ottomans, were superior to the others. The Ottoman Empire committed extremely horrifying deeds, such as murder, rape, and displacement. From 450,000 to 750,000 Pontian Greeks were murdered during the genocide, and about 1.1 million Greek Orthodox Christians from Asia Minor evacuated to Greece in the population exchange of 1923. During that same year, the Hellenistic civilization was removed from Asia Minor.

Salem Witch Trials: Estimated Tens of Thousands Dead

The Salem witch trials occurred in colonial Massachusetts between 1692 and 1693. More than two hundred people were accused of practicing witchcraft—the devil's magic—and twenty were executed. Eventually, the colony admitted the trials were a mistake and compensated the families of those convicted. Since then, the story of the trials has become synonymous with paranoia and injustice. Several centuries ago, many practicing Christians, and those of other religions, had a strong belief that the devil could give certain people, known as witches, the power to harm others, in return for their loyalty. A witchcraft craze rippled through

Europe from the 1300s to the end of the 1600s. Tens of thousands of supposed witches—mostly women—were executed. Though the Salem trials occurred just as the European craze was winding down, local circumstances would explain their onset.

In 1689, English rulers William and Mary started a war with France in the American colonies. Known as King William's War to colonists, it ravaged regions of upstate New York, Nova Scotia, and Quebec, sending refugees into the county of Essex and, specifically, Salem Village in the Massachusetts Bay Colony. (Salem Village is present-day Danvers, Massachusetts; colonial Salem Town became what's now Salem.)

Displaced people created a strain on Salem's resources. This aggravated the existing rivalry between families with ties to the wealth of the port of Salem and those who still depended on agriculture. Controversy also brewed over Reverend Samuel Parris, who became Salem Village's first ordained minister in 1689, but was disliked because of his rigid ways and greedy nature. The Puritan villagers believed all the quarreling was the work of the devil.

In January of 1692, Reverend Parris's daughter Elizabeth, age nine, and niece Abigail Williams, age eleven, started having "fits." They screamed, threw things, uttered peculiar sounds, and contorted themselves into strange positions. A local doctor blamed the supernatural. Another girl, Ann Putnam, age eleven, experienced similar episodes. On February 29, under pressure from magistrates Jonathan Corwin and John Hathorne, the girls blamed three women for afflicting them: Tituba, the Parris's Caribbean slave; Sarah Good, a homeless beggar; and Sarah Osborne, an impoverished elderly woman.

Exercise

Take out a sheet of paper or open a new document on your
computer. For each of the above-described tragedies and crimes
against humanity, write out in your own words what you believe
the thoughts were that drove the acts of destruction. What were the
people thinking? Include both your legitimate and not-so-legitimate
ideas and opinions. It is imperative to be able to look at a situation
from the point of view of a neutral mind's eye in order to develop
truthful discernment. This allows you to place yourself in the shoes
of both sides: the aggressors and the victims. Write out exactly
what you believe they were thinking and feeling at the time. Then,
compare this information to current-day issues around the world,
applying the same techniques of truthful discernment.

> One must aid and assist not only the broken but
> also those who committed the crimes against them;
> for, it is only through love and mercy for all that
> transformative and lasting change can occur.
>
> —MindScope Seven

The Price of Freedom

> It is for freedom that Christ has set us free. Stand
> firm, then, and do not be encumbered once more by
> a yoke of slavery.
>
> —Galatians 5:1 (BSB)

We must consciously choose our own pain in
solutions, or the enemy will decide our price to pay;
faulty thinking will trick you into the belief of a
pain-free path, when there is none. We demonstrate
wisdom and suffer far less by choosing the price

we can afford to pay, and then understanding its
requirements.

—MindScope Seven

Remember, time heeds no man. It is a gift to us, for choosing its
best use. We must be conscientious in recognizing a window of
opportunity when it presents itself. I am talking about the big-
breakthrough type of opportunities, not necessarily attached to
money, although it can be. Opportunity for whatever the most
critical thing needed for the time or circumstance. We must also
be able to act on it in meaningful and effective ways. We must not
merely stand in confusion, questioning and frozen.

The critical ability of understanding and seizing opportunity can
be learned. Opportunity for breakthroughs always presents itself
in stormy conditions. Don't fear the storm! Instead, focus on its
detection well in advance of its development, and then you will be
able to navigate it properly. We can limit its damage and harness its
possibilities through understanding and new approaches. Then, the
storm can be directed most effectively for changing the landscape
of your choosing.

When we aren't successful at harnessing our minds, we also will
not be able to harness everything else that life throws at us. We
often allow the storms to rumble and roll across our landscape,
destroying whatever they choose to, just as Beatrix did for many
years. Even when submitting, Beatrix still understood that people
usually do the opposite of what is needed, thereby feed the fury
in the storms. She learned how to harness the storm brewed
against her and redirect the storm's path, using its fury against the
oppressors. She also knew that her opponents did not understand
this technique. Beatrix took what she knew and, constantly
perfecting her approach, honed her skill and level of accuracy. She

had an amazing ability of reading the landscape around her, no matter where she found herself.

Once you change your approach, just as Beatrix did, there will be no storm you cannot navigate and then direct the change of your choosing. Think correctly. Fight correctly. Develop new approaches. Find new tools. It won't be easy, but you can do it! By creating the tools needed, you can guide your future, building it on a solid foundation.

> The ability to clearly visualize the end game, and **understand** the landscape accurately, will enable you to **conquer** and **succeed**.
>
> —MindScope Seven

Let's begin to take a deeper look at where the inability of proper discernment has led us. Ask yourself, What is the most critical, pressing thing at this time? I'll bet your answer will be one or more of the dreadful conditions of the world today: the violence, hate, drugs, and terrorism destroying our communities and the world around us. We are further threatened by the looming threat of economic decline, job loss, market crashes, banking instability, threats of world and racial wars, and broken families. We are suffering from a loss of foundation, morals, and ethics of humankind overall. So, what's going on in society beneath the surface and at the root of our sickness and downward spiral? This is a most difficult question for all people to ponder, yet finding the answer is a process that should start with a daily routine of checking yourself in relation to your position in the world around you. It is tough for any of us to look in the mirror and embrace our true self, in part because of all the conflicting information we have received up to this point. Some of us know we have been drastically misunderstood and underestimated, and no spoken words would ever convince those around us differently. And then some have been defined to be more than they are capable of being, and the system around them offers sufficient protection and comfort, so there is no advantage in revealing the true self. At this moment, depending on your age, cultural roots, family of origin, gender, race, and even religious beliefs, your ideas of yourself may be very altered, even untrue. Since childhood, you have been receiving labels and placed in boxes of confinement and control. You may be telling yourself it isn't so, but, trust me, it is. We even take on a facade for ourselves to protect the more vulnerable authentic self underneath. There are times when this can be wise and strategically beneficial, but the problem is when you begin to believe the labels others have placed upon you to be the truth. You will begin acting out these labels' definitions or shutting down your true self completely. This can be a tough truth to face, but it is also the route to freedom and solutions you desperately need. You will never find the guiding light and balancer for yourself while living out a facade. And this is no simple mishap; it will change your choice of spouse or significant other, your choice of career, your choice of friends, and your overall success in life. If not corrected, it will impact your children and many generations after you. It is impossible to unlock your mind to new ways of thinking and approaching situations when you aren't operating in an authentic mode. It is necessary to understand yourself in relation to the world in order to access new information for conquering the hauntings of the past, as well as whatever life throws at you in the present. So, with the opportunity of time we must ask, what has the past taught us? Where are we now? How can we best use the gift of time? How can we recognize and harness the opportunities around us right now? In every problem lies the opportunity for solution.

> When I was a child, I spoke as a child, I understood
> as a child, I thought as a child; but when I became
> a man, I put away childish things.
> —1 Corinthians 13:11 (NKJV)

The Ten Commandments (Exodus 20:2–17 NKJV)

I am the Lord your God, who brought you out of the land of Egypt, out of the house of bondage. You shall have no other gods before Me.

You shall not make for yourself a carved image, or any likeness of anything that is in heaven above, or that is in the earth beneath, or that is in the water under the earth; you shall not bow down to them nor serve them. For I, the Lord your God, am a jealous God, visiting the iniquity of the fathers on the children to the third and fourth generations of those who hate Me, but showing mercy to thousands, to those who love Me and keep My Commandments.

You shall not take the name of the Lord your God in vain, for the Lord will not hold him guiltless who takes His name in vain.

Remember the Sabbath day, to keep it holy. Six days you shall labor and do all your work, but the seventh day is the Sabbath of the Lord your God. In it you shall do no work: you, nor your son, nor your daughter, nor your male servant, nor your female servant, nor your cattle, nor your stranger who is within your gates. For in six days the Lord made the heavens and the earth, the sea, and all that is in them, and rested the seventh day. Therefore the Lord blessed the Sabbath day and hallowed it.

Honor your father and your mother, that your days may be long upon the land which the Lord your God is giving you.

You shall not murder.

You shall not commit adultery.

You shall not steal.

You shall not bear false witness against your neighbor.

You shall not covet your neighbor's house; you shall not covet your neighbor's wife, nor his male servant, nor his female servant, nor his ox, nor his donkey, nor anything that is your neighbor's.

Exercise: Create a Written Set of Foundational Rules

Your *rules* should be built on *truths* bigger than your own ideas and opinions. This is your most powerful tool, so give it the time and thought necessary. I used the Ten Commandments as only an example of my truth. Make your own rules based upon your beliefs. Consider making it a laminated wallet-size card, so that it is always with you and accessible when life is tossing your around and you are tempted to allow emotions or society to overwhelm, overcome, and then rule you.

A wise man never assumes the instrument or tool, as definition of self; instead, he carefully selects the most efficient tool for the job, and then swiftly returns to his tool belt for future need.

—MindScope Seven

Chapter 5

Superhero Tools

Tool Belt

The next building block for your battle is the creation of your tool belt. You must press the image of this figurative tool belt into your mind's eye, so that you will be able to access it when needed. Make sure to incorporate a method or process that will help you adapt to this new way of thinking. This is imperative to your success.

Most often, when Beatrix spoke of battles, she also talked about the tools in her tool belt. It wasn't just the words she spoke; it was a mental picture in her mind. She would visually access her tool belt along with her list of foundational rules. These were core tools to her, like a hammer and nails to a carpenter. I questioned Beatrix about how this worked for her. The following is how she described it to me in her own words.

Beatrix

I know this seems harsh and disconnected from humanness, but it has to be. When we are faced with choices or difficult battles, the biggest error I see others make is the attachment to their emotions or ego. This always spells disaster and failure, for themselves and others in their care or presence. And this is even more important when you are dealing with dangerous or particularly delicate situations. You see, when carpenters have a job to do, they choose the right instrument; there is no feeling about it. It's simply about determining which tool in the belt will get the job done in the most efficient way possible. For instance, you don't pull out a screwdriver when you need a hammer. Similarly, you don't throw cotton balls at an enemy when what you need is a hand grenade! You carefully read the landscape, and then you match your efforts and instruments to the reality you face. Errors in your ability to discern and then strategize will lead to great defeat.

In that moment, I got what Beatrix was saying. Her way of visualizing and operating in a mechanical way always took me by surprise and simultaneously confused me. I often thought, *Where did this woman come from?* She then further explained that during this process, not only was she accessing her tool belt visually for the correct tools, she was also balancing it against her foundational rules. This ensured her integrity and moral code for the mission, whatever it might be. If she could not find the balance there, then she would not move further into a plan of execution. At times this created delays for Beatrix, not because of confusion, but because of careful examination of the problem. She spent as much time as needed in the think tank, prayerfully processing the balance and integrity of both tools and foundational rules. As Beatrix explained it, "If strategic ideas or plans contradict foundational rules, you must go back to the drawing board." The only caveat was instruction from the Higher Power, or extreme emergency threatening survival. She understood that God's ways were above and beyond human comprehension. She had learned through experience that if His instructions contradicted logic or societal norms, her actions must be complete obedience and walking in faith.

Exercise

Take time before moving forward to create your own tool belt. This is where you will begin to develop your own tools for battle. Include tools formed around your rules and your strengths. Keep this visual in an obvious place where you can easily access and see it (such as your wallet), until it becomes an automatic mental response. A great place to begin is with your known strengths.

Ninja Ears

Know this, my beloved brothers: let every person be quick to hear, slow to speak, slow to anger.

—James 1:19 (ESV)

A fool takes no pleasure in understanding, but only in expressing his opinion.

—Proverbs 18:2 (ESV)

The easiest men to take out of a room are those with big mouths and big egos!

—MindScope Seven

We use our powerful ears for the weakest actions. The ears are one of the most powerful tools for humans; however, we tend to listen with ill motives and intents. We aren't really listening at all, but, instead, planning our attack. Most of us only listen for lustful reasons. The lust for disagreement, agreement, or acquisitive selfish motives. By doing this, we give our power away. We offer the enemy a gun and bullets, and even cock the trigger, becoming an easy target. No single individual holds all the truth, so listening is imperative for accurate discernment. It is critical to listen, hear, and understand without biases, while actively sifting the information. It requires a disciplined effort to hear without labeling what's familiar. By listening to all parties, the doorway for change begins to crack open. We are all connected, even though we spend countless hours and untold amounts of energy creating division. Listening without speaking yields more information to be unveiled for an individual. Just listen without judgment, without attempting to calculate any solution. Intently absorb the raw information, and then go to your think tank and ponder its meaning. Force yourself to view the information in new and different plausible ways. Only the strong strive to master this skill throughout their lives. Societal norms encourage the opposite, adding more noise and spoken word, without thought. The fear of listening only serves to set us up for failure by limiting ourselves to hearing our own banter. This is a position of weakness.

Great listeners exhibit strength of character. They thrive on listening for understanding and the true power it yields. Keen listening is necessary in the discovery of the truth as well as solutions for all humankind. Remember, a big part of discovering truth is found through contrast of opposing and new ideas. Choosing to listen poses no threat to you, although your mind may be telling you the opposite. Those who refuse to listen will find their well of information to be very shallow, making them extremely weak and easy to defeat. When the time is appropriate in a conversation, you may ask nonthreatening and noninflammatory questions. You do this for the sake of clarifying what you heard and gaining a deeper understanding of the unfamiliar. If you can't manage to do this at first, remain silent until you can. We are all somewhat limited by our own experiences, or lack thereof. We only grow and develop to the extent to which we give ourselves permission to explore new, different, and misunderstood information. We find ourselves in critical time for discernment in society. Listening will be key for unlocking the doors of a better future. We must not allow society, the news, politicians, or other leaders to be our primary source of information. Disallowing yourself this privilege equates to handing your brain over and getting in line with the sheep.

Beatrix was forever performing litmus tests against the things she knew, trying to prove herself wrong. She also welcomed others into this process if they possessed the ability. Her biggest goal was discerning truthfully. She understood the powerful concept of garbage in, garbage out. Most of us try to prove ourselves right; however, Beatrix did the exact opposite. She shared stories of two different occasions that beautifully demonstrate her concept in motion. The first story demonstrates the core values instilled in her children. The second story shows it operating with her employees in the concept of business.

Beatrix with Her Children

I always attempted to prepare my children with the skills and tools I knew their future would require. Part of that lesson, from a very young age, was in teaching them how to skillfully disagree, even with me, their mother. All children play the why-not? card. I just never saw this as negative. You can harbor open communication while you guide them through great teaching moments; or, you can stifle them. But if you do the latter, they will still have the same question, and they will turn to someone else for the answer— and you will have no idea who that someone will be. This leaves a doorway open for another to assume the job of teaching your child core values. This never made sense to me, and I had lived in an environment where you better had not open your mouth. I began to realize that parents do this either for control or inability to substantiate their own ideas and/or words. I always saw this as a problem. My only rule was this: You may question or disagree with anything, but only if done respectfully. However, you had better think before speaking, and you had better sure that you can support your case. I further explained to them that my job would be to tear down their argument, which would also be exactly what they would face in the world. This technique also instilled, at a deeper level, that my children would question things rather than just following sheepishly. That always leads to danger—following sheepishly—and I did not want to set them up for that state of mind. This forced them to be thinkers, absorbers of information, and it taught them how to effectively put details together and then express themselves with effectiveness and respect.

Beatrix with Her Employees

I have always been a stickler for efficient processes, especially in business. Time is money, and time wasted on inefficient methods, or misappropriated energy, costs everyone in the long run. It hurts the business owner's bottom line, it creates problems within the workplace, and it frustrates employees and then the customers. I wanted my employees to spend their time and energy on income-generating and service activities, not fruitless micromanaged busywork. I strongly dislike busywork, finding it insulting and preventative of reaching goals, so I did not want to inhibit my employees with such nonsense. I maintained an open-door communication policy, a safe place to discuss and air their ideas or concerns. I frequently expressed, during sales meetings, that if they had developed a better and more efficient process, we would adopt it. Like my children, they knew they would be up against a challenge, so they were to come prepared for such. In business, it is critical to openly challenge ideas because this is how you develop and grow your business and employees. It also helps employees understand their importance in the overall process. They, along with your customers, are the only reason for the existence of the business. Simply put, they pay your bills. This procedure builds teamwork, and sparks development in employees. Employees will challenge themselves to come up with better ideas, and this in turn will spill over to all areas of their performance.

We, too, could reap benefit from the ninja listening skills of Beatrix. We are immersed in the constant noise of the world. If you cannot train your ears to filter information properly, you will fall for anything, and thereby become unstable in the process of listening and thought. So often, the things reaching ours ears are meant to sway us in a direction, usually having to do with the self-interest of others. Most people absorb without a single question. This is dangerous, and also plays a big role in the incorrect narratives woven against others in society, perhaps even within our families. By becoming a discerning listener, you gain advantage in every situation. And with that advantage, you can create and develop a greater environment for those in your care and around you.

Think Tank

Before moving on to the next step, let's discuss creating your own think tank. This is not some random activity. As you can see by now, the thoughts and actions of Beatrix were methodical and not left to chance or whim. Many people talk about change, and that's part of the problem. They talk but provide no actions to back their words or cause. They become just noise in the atmosphere. Turn your attention to the men or women who courageously hold themselves accountable first, and then turn their words into actions on behalf of their fellow humans. We must be able to detect the useless noise and remove ourselves from it. We must separate the relevant things from this noise, and then take what is relevant to our think tanks. I have basically three different think tanks, all involving physical movement and solitude. While I am in my think tank, I meditate in prayer, asking for the clarity and answers from a power higher than myself. A power that I cannot influence at all, and to which I must adhere in strict obedience. When I am in my think tank, away from the noise and chaos, I can hear the voice commanding my thoughts and actions. It is a time to recondition my heart to a will and force exceeding my own. By doing this procedure over and over on a continual basis, my success in mindful decision-making greatly improves. It is only when I follow a path on my own without following this process, or when I allow the intrusion of some outside influence, that failure and error take control. So, in choosing your own think tank, you must pick activities or places that allow you freedom from the noisy chaos of life. Also, make sure that whatever you choose ignites your inquisitive nature. Open your mind to the broader spectrum and allow all questions to be feasible until proved wrong when checked against your own foundational rules/the truth. So, when you go into this space, you will be prepared for strong debate of the answers you are seeking. But you must also keep your mind completely free from biases or social norms. Do not allow any of your ideas into this space. Clear your mind, creating a quiet space, free from other influences. If you believe in a divine Higher Power, this time is critical for inner spiritual growth. It is important to carefully select both the space and activity that will create the space you need to connect to the inner spiritual self. My preferred spaces are doing an intensive workout, gardening, listening to music, or doing chores around the house. Movement, for me, is imperative; however, your formula may be different. These are just the optimal activities that allow me to enter this space easily and then fully open up to new information that wasn't present before. Understand that you may not get your answers in one session; so, this will require consistent, deliberate, disciplined action on your part.

How blessed is the man who does not walk in the counsel of the wicked, nor stand in the path of sinners, nor sit in the seat of scoffers! But his delight is in the law of the LORD, And in His law, he meditates day and night. He will be like a tree firmly planted by streams of water, which yields its fruit in its season And its leaf does not wither; And in whatever he does, he prospers.

—Psalm 1:1–3 (NASB)

Consider what I say, for the Lord will give you understanding in everything.

—2 Timothy 2:7 (NASB)

Litmus Test

The king said, "Get me a sword." So they brought a sword before the king. The king said, "Divide the living child in two, and give half to the one and half to the other."

—1 Kings 3:24–25 (NASB)

"To split the baby" is a reference to a story in the Old Testament, in Kings 3:5–14, regarding a decision of Solomon that shows his wisdom when given a difficult task. As king, Solomon was often asked to judge between people with difficult problems, and his solutions were considered very wise. The above term is often used to describe an unreasonable solution that may be used as a way to find an underlying truth.

This is very demonstrative of what I call the "methods of Beatrix," which she used in her waking moments throughout the day. She might even have continued performing her elaborate unnoticed tests even while sleeping. This was a part of the very makeup and fiber of her being. I often asked Beatrix, "How do you know all this?" To which she would reply, "I just do; I have always known people and recognized what was to come, even before the action occurred." As Beatrix described it to me, it became especially difficult for her as a child, when she was too young to understand this ability. It made her feel isolated and alone. She had no one with whom she could discuss these things that she intuitively knew—except God, and she did discuss them with Him. Later, these intuitive knowings developed into truth.

Beatrix on Intuition

I found my intuition very frightening and confusing, so I would find ways to test it. Even once I had proved my skills and tested my theories many times over, I would still find another way to test my intuition, attempting to prove it wrong. I wanted to be wrong. I didn't want to see what I saw. But, again and again, my intuitive knowledge proved to be correct. It nearly drove me crazy! It certainly drove me into a world of my own. I hated knowing in advance, having no one to talk to. *Just make it go away!* I would think. Once you see, you can no longer turn a blind eye, if you possess a conscience at all. I was brutally hard on myself. There were times when it assisted me in business, enabling me to maneuver in ways that others didn't understand and allowing me to ably advocate for the people I served. These were my few moments of saving grace with this wicked curse. I would wonder why God had cursed me so, because often He would reveal things but then instruct me to do nothing, or to just take abuse and swallow it down. He would never allow me to take, only to give. At times, when I grew frustrated and even angry, He would give me a firm reminder: "It's not for you!" To which I often inwardly replied, *Why would You make anyone like this, to be abused and misused?* Understand, I am not talking about a few occurrences; this occurred for the entirety of my life, every day. I never understood, at least not until now, why He made me this way and why the path had to be so difficult. I'm now very grateful for His strict discipline and constant reminders throughout the years. Now, being older and wiser, I see that without that interaction, I might have become a very bad person. I possessed the power to do so! That one thought alone inspires me to work harder, because I know that God made more people like me. And, if those people do not know Him, acknowledging Him as the All-Powerful, their paths will surely lead to evil intentions toward humankind. Any power that is not checked is destined to be used for evil. My opponents, the people I had to work against in my fight to advocate for others, were also very smart and powerful. I didn't stand a chance without God; my team was a whopping total of me and Him.

In the many discussions I had with Beatrix, her vivid description of how she performed the litmus test truly left me speechless. It is best described as otherworldly, but she was always humbled by the ability. As we talked about it, it seemed to me that her humbleness grew from fear. She feared the misuse of knowing (intuition) just as much as she feared the knowing itself. She clearly believed in a Higher Power; for her, that was God. She often said, "You know, ignorance truly is bliss!" Her methods might be compared to the ways of King Solomon as described in the Bible.

Key Points in the Process of Beatrix's Litmus Testing

1. Studying the characters and sorting them through a series of paradoxical tests was essential. The tests were never the same, therefore keeping much undetectable to any observers. Long before she began testing, she had a clear understanding of each character, and the real problem, not merely a perceived or stated problem.

2. Operating quietly and under the radar, so as to not call attention to herself or raise alarm, was also imperative. She had an uncanny way of being completely authentic in her approach, yet those she fought against were distracted from any methods she was using. This successfully unarmed people, making her access greater, even vast.

3. Another critical point was that she understood how to get underneath the rooted problem, and she was very patient in her extraction and solutions. She took the time needed, using a careful and methodical approach.

4. Also essential, she always kept her hands clean, so to speak, allowing the guilty parties to create a trap for themselves on their own. She would literally tell them exactly what she was about, including her intentions. But because of how they had labeled her, they completely dismissed her. She described this as "building them an escape hatch." By this, she meant allowing them to choose door number one or door number two, while she patiently observed and calculated strategy. By this time, in her execution of strategy, there really was only one viable option for them. The smart ones willingly made the right choice for themselves, remaining unscathed. By subtly and patiently building the escape hatch, problems were resolved without harm to anyone. The goal was to correct the problem, unnoticed. This allowed all parties to maintain dignity, and it also kept open the opportunity for unity of the conflicting parties.

Of critical importance, she was fair and honest with all parties. Her goal and methods were never about destruction, but, rather, *change*, in the sense of just and fair treatment. She understood the importance of bringing people together, so that no one would be harmed. If harm came to anyone, it was a willful choice by that person, an act of individual defiance. Beatrix understood that defiance by any person leads to destruction, and it is always best to deter people from such a path. She could bring the so-called villains and victims to peaceful understanding and resolution. In most cases, no one ever knew what she had done. She took no credit. She understood that when you try to get credit and seek visibility, it undermines success of the whole mission. Her goal was to complete the mission and then walk away.

Thought Processor: "This" or "That" Thinking

Solution-based thinking is not the same thing as black-and-white thinking. Black-and-white thinking is most commonly based on a set of rules set by an organization, and these rules often change throughout time. This is one reason why problems go unsolved for lengthy periods of time. It is also the thinking that breeds the mentality of "it's the principal of the matter." This very simple mind-set is nearly impossible for most people to adjust in order to allow change to occur. Beatrix operated in solution-based thoughts and actions, rather than emotions or societal rules. Instead, her focus was always on the future outcomes. She carefully assessed the methods of application in each situation. Her focus was centered on successful outcomes and the most efficient process to achieve the desired results. This caused much confusion and questions about her motives. It often put her in a negative light, but she refused methods that did not work or that could lead others astray. This was where her so-called nasty little curse would bite her once again. She understood what the variety of outcomes would be and what she needed to do to protect others from harm. Beatrix was not looking to break rules; she showed great regard and respect for the rules, until such time as they proved dysfunctional or damaging to people. She understood that most rules were in place for specific reasons and to keep orderly processes. However, when she saw a rule or process that hurt people, or lacked functional purpose, changing them became her goal. This was only on matters of significance, not frivolous things for emotional needs. She would take the appropriate channels regarding authority, to plead her case, provide evidence for the effectiveness of another process and show how it would be more beneficial for all parties. She took her time in careful study and preparation before even mentioning anything about change. She understood a very basic concept in regard to change: It is *always* either "this" or "that." For example, a person wants to get into shape but doesn't want to change eating habits or commit to an exercise regimen. They want "this" (getting into shape), but they keep doing "that" (eating poorly and not exercising). If you want "this," you must do "that" in order to produce it. So, Beatrix would quickly assess what needed to be done, sorting through her choices and eliminating the ones that did not lead to the desired results. For Beatrix, this was a very fast and extremely accurate mental process. It's "this" or "that," and then you choose what you really want, and act on it.

Menu Board

Now it's time to process the information collected from your think tank. You may be back in your think tank before the processing begins. This is something I usually do inside my think tank. In each step of the thought or action process, I first have a visual. This isn't something that I attempt to create; instead, it is just a natural process for me. Do not take that lightly; be certain to put this in your process as well. Visuals are so very important to execute anything successfully. You must first be able to see it in your mind's eye. If this doesn't come naturally to you, be sure to make it a new skill and then add it to your tool belt. I usually give myself three to four viable options. Let me emphasize that the options you place on your visual menu board must be viable options. Place them in an ABC order and then begin dissecting outcomes. If you are performing this step correctly, it should not be an overall quick process. Perhaps, you will quickly discard one or two of the options, based on your check against your foundational rules. You can cross off those options. You may ask, Why put them on the board at all? You put them on the board because they are viable options for the given situation. Perhaps you cannot even cross anything off initially, meaning that you must work through each scenario. So how do you work through the options? You begin by taking one option at a time, and then following it through to the end result. Observe the end results carefully, including how to deal with each of the characters involved. We will discover more about how to understand the characters, according to their personalities and any other influences around them. This type of information becomes vital in discovering the systematic process around thinking and behaviors. And, then understanding how that process, or lack thereof, dictates outcomes. This is a most critical part of the process. If you did not complete the beginning steps, any solutions derived will be inaccurate. Keep in mind that if something comes up during this process pointing to information that you don't understand, or requires more investigation, abort, and go back to the drawing board. Simply put, back up a few steps, and gain what you need for accuracy. You must have all necessary information to derive the (1) worst-possible outcomes, and (2) best-possible outcomes. Always plan for the worst and hope for the best. It's perfectly fine to have emergency plans that you never need to use. This is no place for dreamy wishes, only cold hard facts. If you are moving along productively, continue the process of elimination until you have determined which option holds the reasonable solution and you have filtered in all outcomes. Once you engage in the chosen option, there is little room for error, and you are bound to face some challenges. There are no error-proof plans, even when you do your best in the planning process. A wrench will come from nowhere and be tossed right in the middle of your plan. The goal is to plan for everything, and the more you practice this method, the more refined your process will become. So, in your assessment, be brutally honest in determining what you can live with, and the consequences you can accept, before proceeding.

Your Voice

> Those who consider themselves religious and yet
> do not keep a tight rein on their tongues deceive
> themselves, and their religion is worthless.
>
> —James 1:26 (NIV)

> For in many things we offend all. If any man offend
> not in word, the same is a perfect man, and able also
> to bridle the whole body.
>
> —James 3:2 (KJV)

The voice provides both function and pleasure for us, yet it remains one of the most ineffectively used instruments of humankind. Most all of us enjoy music daily and hear people talk all day long. Need I even explain which one is pleasure and which is pain? And then, there are those looking to thieve our voice and reshape it for their purpose. You know, like politicians or religious leaders assuring us that they are working on the side of protecting humanity. I don't even think further explanation is needed here to describe how they have actively misused and abused the trust of the people they claim to serve. This demonstrates a great point for us in terms of the importance of never giving your voice away. Guard it well, not just for what you might say but also for what others might falsely accuse you of saying.

How can we learn to lasso our tongues and harness our voice as an effective tool? The bad guys know this game well, but we keep falling for their games, trusting them with all we have. I am amazed at the phenomenon of how people supply what the bad guy needs to take them down. Yet the good guy who would protect them, they would slay on the spot. Why? The two most important culprits of hindrance are ego (pride) and emotions. In several different passages, the Bible explains to us just how difficult it is to bridle one's tongue; but if we succeed there first, we will also succeed at reining in the entire body. We have programmed ourselves for accepting standards of society, in seeking pleasure and opportunity in the shiny fake objects while deny the authentic. Earlier, we looked at tragedies against humanity that would have never occurred without a compelling and convincing voice to lure the people into an intrinsic state of blindly following the leader. One of the best examples is Adolf Hitler. I have studied almost everything possible about this horrifying leader. He certainly understood how to use his voice effectively, but in disgustingly evil ways. How could one individual lead others in the brutality that followed, executing horrible acts against innocent people? Through fear, one man successfully convinced those he ruled to carry out the murders of more than seventeen million people. Do we think, somehow, that we are much smarter and so it could never happen to us? This is a dangerous thought pattern. We see good, honest people yield to the power of evil leaders and evildoers. Their targets are usually innocent beings who aren't willing to conform to their power and desires. So, the evil set out tongues of fire to control, or even rid themselves of, any opposition. And, perfectly good people go along with this, because the evil ones' silvery tongues lick out exactly what their hearts desire. The people then swallow the deceptive words and the ugliness to follow, feeding what their ego and emotions desire, in lieu of anything valuable or true. This is a shortsighted and costly perspective.

So, how do we make our voices work for us and others who may be suffering? It is probably not as you would think, joining some group, or gathering in the street with signs. While this may have had some success in the past, we must weigh in our current conditions or situations needing attention. We must carefully size up our opponents and the landscape in order to come up with a strategy for the best use of voice.

Beatrix Finds Her Voice

Silent no more! I can't even count the number of times this phrase has repeated in my mind since the day my mother passed away. The more time passed, the clearer this simple statement became to me. It wasn't just my mom's voice; it was also the voices of any people who'd ever had their voices thieved from them. It is no easy task to take one's voice back, especially after years of oppression. The lines between truth and lies begin to mesh together, becoming believable and accepted truth. The victims become confused in the brainwashing methods they are exposed to, as their own truths and voices fade slowly into the background. The narrative of the puppet masters slowly deludes their thinking, making it too difficult to fight for extended periods and far easier to accept the alternative narrative. Victims become tired, so very tired. As I observed my mother throughout the years, I could see her slip away more and more. It was heartbreaking. And she loved my father so very much; I know she probably held the same false hope that I held for so many years. This is how people become brainwashed, even by people who supposedly love them. But I could always see it. That is not to say that I didn't have the same struggle, because I did. I continually worked at separating the truth of my authentic self from the designed narrative applied to me.

By this time, I had known Beatrix for some time. I had watched her struggle to sort out the demons still haunting her from the past. Beatrix was very skilled at creating narratives for the very people who had abused and misused her. She created narratives to protect her oppressors and stay attached to them. We discussed this on many occasions. But she always explained it to me as *hope*. She really hoped that those who abused her would have an awakening, and there would be a happily-ever-after outcome. Sadly, this didn't happen. I must admit, at times, I didn't know if Beatrix would make it over this hurdle and discover a new life, the life that had been stolen from her so many years ago.

Shortly after her mother's passing, Beatrix was explaining some recent occurrences within her family. Beatrix had no one to support her, so it was easy for her to continue accepting bad circumstances and treatment. Beatrix needed to connect with her anger, rather than burying herself as unimportant. She rarely allowed her anger when it came to people she loved or felt loyal to. Beatrix wanted a family so badly that I think she would have found a similar fate as her mother, if I didn't help her push through this hurdle. So, I told her, "Beatrix, if there were ever a time to get mad, it is now. You have to get mad, Beatrix! Be the person you are in business. Be that woman; for if you don't, they are going to destroy you!"

Beatrix later told me how important these statements became for her finding freedom. She was forever the calm, stoic, mysterious woman. You could never get a read on her. You could never check her pulse, so to speak. She only allowed a few trusted people to see her real self. Beatrix finally allowed herself to accept the anger, and then she used that connection as a guide to her truthful reality, even with those she loved. It took that for Beatrix. It takes that for any person who has faced oppression or abuse for extended periods. They have been silenced for so long, forced to play roles assigned to them, that those observing believe the untruthful reality. It isn't a choice in these situations because the consequences are very real, and very dangerous. It's maddening for them, nearly driving them out of their minds. Living in a parallel universe would drive anyone mad. The weaker they become, the stronger the hold the perpetrators gain on them. The perpetrator sets out false narratives against their victims to bring a belief that their victims are crazy or evil. This allows the perpetrator to bask in a more positive light, as a hero of sorts. You must realize how consciously aware the perpetrator is of exactly how to orchestrate this madness.

Individuals who seek to take another's voice see people as chattel, not as human beings. They always carefully select those closest to them, or those weaker, in order to have individuals who are agreeable and naturally willing to serve others.

Beatrix was never confused by the dynamics; well, at least, she hadn't been for a very long time. Instead, she was just forever hopeful to maintain relationships with the very ones who had harmed her. She wanted to believe the lies they told her, placing herself as the responsible party needing adjustment. The responsibility didn't bother her; she would have done anything possible to be loved and accepted by these people. Each time she took their bait, she found herself tricked again, heartbroken once again. I think letting go of the false hope, and the toxic relationships, might have been impossible if the series of events had not unfolded. We will never know this for sure. But, after her mother's passing, and a series of other devastating events, Beatrix got mad. Real mad! And her anger brought a new awareness she had never known.

Anger

> It is wiser to *use* anger, rather than to ignore it. Anger can be masterfully transformed to create the change needed for conquering that which created the anger or affliction.
>
> —MindScope Seven

It's important to understand that Beatrix was a God-fearing woman, a spiritual woman. She described to me later what the anger looked like when it began to crawl from her insides.

Beatrix on Anger

I felt such ferocious built-up rage. I felt like I was going to explode. There were times it scared me. It was overwhelming, and I didn't want anyone to be hurt. I had tried to contain the rage in a tiny compartment on the inside. This destroys a person, and it comes out in some way. I finally let it out. In private, I screamed, yelled, and cursed those who had hurt me. I allowed my voice to be heard outside of my body. I usually just visualized the people and told them exactly what I thought. The anger, hurt, and pain that others had inflicted on me was destroying me from the inside out. I am embarrassed about it, but somehow it was the only way to get it outside of my body. It felt great, like a therapy of sorts, instant relief and mind clearing. I felt bad about it, but with the madness swirling around me, especially in the most difficult times, I needed enough strength to stand firm and not go backwards. Abusers are great at breaking you down, and the abused learn to be abused without questioning it. They learn to accept the abuse, to survive. I learned to look at my cursing as an instrument in my tool belt. Each time I felt weak, I would whip it out of the holster, and this helped me unleash my inner strength to endure. It also helped me stay connected to truth, rather than the narrative the abusers had beat into my soul. I knew I wouldn't need it forever, but I needed it now, or I would go back, I would allow them to finish me off. I had to keep giving myself permission to be angry, and look at the facts as they really were, instead of what the abuser had made me believe for so long. I knew I would soon be able to remove this tool and toss it in the trash, which seemed a great resting place for a trash mouth! Once I was able to connect to the anger and reality as it was, I realized that my abusers had given me the very strength I would need to fight them. I must admit to getting a little sick pleasure from that. I was actually doing it, walking toward my freedom—or, perhaps, death—it didn't much matter to me anymore. I knew that I could not live whatever time I might have left in the same as I'd lived the first near fifty years; I would end up just like my mother. I made up my mind to keep going, even if it killed me. I was always strong; but at that point, I had never felt weaker in my life. How would I ever fight this battle when I felt so weak and sick? So, I would plug back into the anger, and then I would review my history in my mind—or state out it loud—just so I could be strong enough to what I had to do. "No, Beatrix!" I would say to myself when their toxic words engulfed my mind like waves violently crashing down. "No, Beatrix, that is not true! They are lying to you again; this is what really happened." Would I be strong enough to stand, strong enough to keep putting one foot in front of the other, when I didn't know where my next meal would come from or how I would pay my bills? I asked God to forgive me. In those difficult moments, when I didn't even want to live anymore, I would have to remind myself of the actual truth, and I would begin speaking it out loud, if needed. I couldn't allow their narrative in my head; I couldn't let them trick me again.

So often, victims of abuse are silenced. Abuse happens within families, but it can also be to the result of issues with gender, race, or religion. The effects are all the same. As you can see in her own words, Beatrix often operated outside her body, but this was also how she finally overcame being victimized. Beatrix learned how to take each tool that her abusers used against her and turn it on them in her fight for her long-overdue freedom. We will look in more detail at the specifics of exactly how Beatrix was able to execute her process, even with the odds completely against her, even while broken and sick. Beatrix was a survivor, a fighter. She had spent years fighting and advocating for others, but she couldn't seem to fight the battle for herself. She finally took the gutsy approach needed to break through the toxic systems used to confine her. She used her anger brilliantly, constructively, and methodically to gain ground and overcome the opposition, while never being vindictive against them.

She told me, "You can never act vindictively. You must always keep your hands clean; this is a hard-line rule that should never be broken."

Beatrix allowed her abusers to choose the fight, the weapons, and then masterfully won the battle they started, using against them the very weapons they wielded when harming her. How was Beatrix able to take lifelong struggles from abusive environments and transform them into strength used in overcoming? She took what is usually perceived to be weakness and turned it into her weapons for victory.

There is often a confusing phenomenon that occurs with victims of any type of oppression or abuse. After a time, they either submit to the oppression and lose themselves, or they fight back with what they have. We never know what people carry around with them, or the boiling pot brewing within them. We often take for granted our own life, with little understanding or care of the reality others may be enduring. We have no way of predicting or controlling outcomes of those who have experienced the cruelest side of the world and people. The platform of choices for the individuals who have suffered atrocities is nothing like that of a more traditional well-functioning family. We sometimes want to write it off as a simple decision of right and wrong. There is no argument about certain things being right or wrong, such a stealing, murder, bullying, and many forms of abuse. Even those who choose the wrong path understand that they are doing wrong, except for a rare few. The problem becomes more about: (1) other choices that might be available for them in their unique position (possible blockers include money, location, lack of retraining, education, and overhauling of ideas, beliefs, and patterns); and (2) the resources available to provide a support system for the difficult task of overcoming the past and creating a healthy, functioning life (possible blockers include dysfunctional relationships pulling them back by means of systematic rejection from labeling and ostracization). These are just a few of the underlying roots that have allowed crime and drugs to overrun our streets and now our families. What was once a smaller and more manageable problem has now reached epidemic proportions. Even supposed well-functioning families are seeing the results bleeding into the structure of their homes, as we see record-breaking numbers of parents addicted to prescription drugs, alcohol, and recreational drugs. For many may be the model citizen in their communities, but, behind closed doors, it's a war zone. In this group we see a broad spectrum of people from various socioeconomic levels and the types of drugs seen as acceptable even by those in positions of leadership. So, the drug of choice is different, based on their perceived status or their beliefs.

This, too, became a shock to Beatrix as she explained the decline of her mother leading up to her death.

Beatrix on Her Mother's Addiction

Mom was addicted to pills. From as early as I can remember, there was a vast amount of prescription drugs in our home. As a child, I thought nothing of it, because the medications were prescribed by doctors. It wasn't until I was a teenager that I began to recognize it as a problem. As our home continued in violence and passive-aggressive control tactics, my mother seemed to have more trouble with coping. As I grew older, I would try to talk about what was going on in our home, and this would always result in her getting very angry and then placing guilt on me and my siblings in attempt to regain order and control and maintain the cover-up. She would even deny the events that occurred, as if we were lying about them. Our parents would deliberately create divisions between all of the siblings, because they needed to keep everyone full of mistrust and upset in order to maintain their same level of control as we got older.

The cycle would continue round and round, as division and animosity grew between everyone. Each of my siblings and I suffered different fates within the family structure, as we each were assigned our own place within the unit, and no one dared step out of line. This continued even once we were adults, because the consequences would be so severe. It worked like any other dysfunctional system of power: There is always one person assigned a position of close alignment with the dysfunctional leader. The person chosen for this role will be the one most easily controlled and agreeable to the one(s) in power, even if the chosen one doesn't agree inwardly. Then, there must be one perceived to be the "bad guy," the one who isn't aligned or in agreement with what's happening. I was that person in the family structure. The remainder of siblings will either be placed into one of these two categories or ignored completely. Our family fell under the category of a glass-house image. This became a particularly difficult fraud to uphold in the community, on account of the happenings behind closed doors. We then had to put on the smiles for the congregation and community of my father's church, acting like the perfect family. Living out this lie, and maintaining the boxes we were forced into, became more than we all could bear.

As my mother's prescription-drug habit grew, she became a different person; it was almost impossible to have a conversation with her. Before her death, she would frequently fall over on the church pew; nevertheless, all was still hidden and brushed over. My mother was riddled with guilt by this time, as she felt responsible for so much that had occurred. It is such a vicious cycle for each person involved. As the guilt ate at her, so did her prescription-drug habit. My mother was a victim of long-term abuse that she could not exit; my father would have destroyed her life if she had even attempted to leave. She truly had no way out, and she was surrounded by a community who worshipped our father, so no one would have even believed her if she had told the truth. He used the pulpit to keep the control strings on his congregation, and on his family as well, carefully weaving narratives that set him up as godlike, and my mother as stupid or bothersome to him. The members of the congregation were so taken with him that they would just laugh along, as I watched my mother shrink into the pew, the hurt crawling deeper inside of her.

Oftentimes, people say, "Why don't people in these situations just leave?" I can tell you with certainty, that was never an option for my mother. He was sick and crazy enough to do anything. She attempted to leave when we were younger, and it only led to more danger. The abuse was no occasional event: it was constant and purposeful, and he was a preacher. How does anyone navigate these waters? We were all fed the narrative of how our responsibility to his ministry was ordained by God. It was beyond difficult being forced to live in such conditions and cover for the one who was destroying us all. No one in the community would have believed or assisted us. People much prefer to deny when such things are happening; or, they don't want to get involved for fear of consequences in their own lives. This decline that I hoped I would escape continued throughout my adult life and then filtered through to my own children.

From Beatrix's story, we can see an example of the vast and unexpected affects that occur when misaligned and malignant power labels its victims, then holds them hostage for a lifetime through alienation by the puppet master who wishes to keep them confined and under control. We are watching the world unravel before our eyes daily, while our greater outlying enemies are sharpening their claws, watching the inward fighting of humanity playing out, waiting for the perfect time to strike. As we have accepted definitions with little question or thought, it has easily nudged all of humankind into the position of brother against brother. We are seeing this in families and communities all over the world. Those who are hurting are ripe for the picking by those who have evil intentions. As families have continued to decline into brokenness, leaving no safe place for the children residing within the walls of their own homes. This problem has now spilled into all our lives, even though ideas of "us" and "them" were so carefully crafted. There are no true dividers in human suffering. When part of humankind collectively suffers, it eventually reaches all our doorsteps, in unimaginable ways. As we continue on our journey, we will see how Beatrix was able to beat the odds not only for her family but also in extension to a much greater problem than people could imagine. Paradoxically, she did this using the very labels and boxes of confinement meant to break her and hold her hostage.

Beatrix on Faith

"God uses all events and struggles that one of us may encounter, for the benefit of all." It took some time on my frightening journey of faith to realize that God was going to take my past trials, and my current circumstances, and entangle them in such a way as to assist a much bigger problem of many. I realize now that by drawing me into a battle for the love and protection of my own child, He was able to use that for a bigger plan, and for many more. I do not have the appropriate words to explain what God has faithfully brought me through. I am even grateful for all of the suffering because I know without a doubt that my entire life was being shaped early on for the very function that God would need me for later in life. If I would have known all of the dangers up front, I probably couldn't have made the walk of faith. What I knew for sure, though, was the love for my own child, and that I would fight man or beast for his return to safety. As I went deeper into the problem, He revealed more and more to me … things I never wanted to know. I can only explain it as a deeply intimate relationship, none like I had ever known with God before. A completely new discovery of relating with God.

So, as we are trying to untangle the abuses of one another, we must not encourage the victims to hide or repress their feelings or become pressured by outsiders to take on a narrative to protect the oppressor. Instead, victims need safe and constructive ways of processing the events and emotions, from the past or present, without pressure of creating a more comfortable narrative for the sake of comforting others or the perpetrator. Giving ourselves permission to reveal our own truth, and grieve our losses, opens the door to the future. We then finally become able to lay down the hurts from the past, and then we can walk through the door to the future.

Some phenomena associated with living with abuse are described below.

Anger: Survivors of abuse may feel intense anger at their abusers, at those who knew of the abuse and failed to intervene, and even at themselves for being abused, particularly when they believe they could or should have stopped it. Anger is a natural and normal response to being abused, and survivors can learn to manage their anger in a constructive manner that will facilitate healing.

Dissociation: Lack of feeling, numbness, confusion, and out-of-body experiences may occur during or after abuse to help the victim avoid the pain and fear associated with the abuse. In rare cases, memories of abuse may be repressed, and some victims may not have any conscious memory of the abuse.

Shame: Guilt and shame are often experienced by survivors who believe they deserved the abuse, were responsible for it, or failed to stop it. Challenging these beliefs can help survivors of abuse and oppression transform these feelings.

Self-Destructive Behavior: Sometimes survivors will self-medicate, with drugs or alcohol, for example, or engage in self-harm, such as burning or cutting themselves. Other times, people may seek out scenarios in which the abuse is repeated, neglect their personal health and hygiene, or sabotage any potential for success. These behaviors are often representative of low self-esteem, which is a common symptom of abuse.

Trust Issues: Learning to trust others after abuse has occurred can be challenging.

> Silence is either golden or deadly; one must understand the difference between the two, the when and how.
>
> —MindScope Seven

Laser Vision, Neutral Lens

> In their case the god of this world has blinded the minds of the unbelievers, to keep them from seeing the light of the gospel of the glory of Christ, who is the image of God.
>
> —2 Corinthians 4:4 (ESV)

> "Ask, and it will be given to you; seek, and you will find; knock, and it will be opened to you."
>
> —Matthew 7:7 (ESV)

To reach becoming a superhero with our own God-given talents and abilities it must be accompanied by keen discernment of the needs and proper use of those very skills. True understanding is only accomplished through a laser-type vision. This allows us to see beneath the surface and through imitations of truth. How do we gain laser vison? Begin by laying down your own personal views, opinions, biases, and cultural upbringing. This is imperative for making correct assessments and having the ability to see through the deceptive and confusing images we are fed daily. Most of us gobble down only the obvious, rarely questioning anything, because that is the easier way. Most afford themselves this luxury of an easier path and a lazy existence. What they don't realize, and aren't planning for, is the inevitability of future outcomes produced from that mind-set. They prefer the path of least resistance, or the road that benefits them at that time. While the surface view is easier and built for instant gratification, truthful thinking yields long-term positives. We live in a world that is full of lust, ever demanding of instant gratification.

Images create patterns in our minds that helps us make connections to emotions, ideas, and decisions. Those images become moments of nostalgia. We see something, and our brains light up with all types of sensory stimuli, and we begin to make judgments. When we become complacent in this thought pattern, assumptions take over, even tricking us about what our eyes saw or what the underlying truth is. This way of intaking information makes us blind to the truth, believing it is unimportant, even evil. We may even confuse bad with good.

Our minds begin taking on assumptions, just like muscle memory when you exercise. In exercise, the muscles remember what you have taught them, and if you keep repeating the same movements, the muscles are no longer challenged; as a result, growth and definition stop. To maintain and keep growing, you must keep changing your workout routine, so the muscles are forced to work for you as you place new demands on them. They can't just hang out in your body in a state of complacency. If you allow that for too long, you lose muscle mass, perhaps even leading to injuries in the aging process. The muscles have diminished, because there is no demand to keep them functioning, much less growing. When I talk about laser vision, of course it has a little to do with the eyes, and more with the sorting of what the eyes take in; it is about looking for the things unseen.

I'm sure you have experienced, on occasion, being in a group of people where every person seemed to view the exact same thing differently. The thing viewed remained constant; however, everyone perceived it differently. The results of what the people saw and comprehended varied. Why is that? All people have been conditioned in certain ways, and this changes how we see things, as well as our beliefs about those things. Few people take the time to deconstruct what they see or know, and the meaning of it. Earlier, I explained a few processes used by Beatrix to break things down to the very root of the matter, seeking the truth. For Beatrix, this is second nature; her mind immediately begins the process, because this is part of her natural makeup. She is always searching for the truth; putting herself under as many litmus tests as possible, attempting to prove herself wrong. This is an unusual response for most when intaking information. Most people have learned that they must be right! Most people take what they see at face value, or through the perception of others. Beatrix understood that face value rarely spells truth. Our perspectives are also partially formed through the generational impact of the time when we were born and the ideas of that time. So, I asked Beatrix, "When forming judgments of the patterns you formulate through the process of litmus tests, aren't you really just predicting the current trends of the day?" To which, she boldly replied, "Absolutely not!"

Her detailed explanation of her above reply appears below.

Beatrix on Seeing Truth

I never weigh truth against trends, because trends change with time and generations, rendering them unreliable sources of truth. Truth stands the course of time, never changing; so, if you can make the connection to truth, then you can apply the patterns for proper discernment. Once you have the core principles of truth, they can be used over and over again for proper discernment. You can then free up time for calculating new information and filling your belt with better and stronger tools. The efficiency that truth offers for planning and results saves time and effort the next time you're faced with a similar problem. If you rely on trends, as soon as the trend fades, everything you know becomes useless information. I recognize trends, but I think of them as trends, not truth, because they can change on a dime, making your efforts worthless and wasteful. Consequently, I get out my so-called neutral goggles before beginning any assessment process. I focus on the things unseen or attempting to hide. I begin testing all the information, looking for flaws in my own assessments. I test in as many ways needed. I change up my testing formats as many times needed to get to the truth I seek. My methods are as different as the individuals that I may be dealing with at the time.

The more Beatrix described some of the elaborate, difficult tests she performed, the more it left me speechless and at times a bit frightened. I kept thinking, *Is she testing me?* I knew the answer: of course she was! She made me feel raw and vulnerable, but this was one of the keys to her success. She wanted the rawest of information, and she put herself in very vulnerable positions to get it. So, I consider myself to be a pretty sharp cookie, but she had stopped me cold in my tracks, right when I thought I had an aha moment. Beatrix never minded any of my questions or challenges; she even liked them. Somehow, she took them as an opportunity to sharpen her own thinking and skills. She had great respect for anyone seeking the truth, and she enjoyed offering new nuggets for her rich bank of knowledge. She really enjoyed and appreciated conversations of debating ideas with a person who would work at solidly proving the argument in question. She knew this process might reveal something she had not yet discovered. She was always seeking new information. She held a clear understanding that no single person could hold the absolute truth and that others held the details not yet discovered. She studied topics from the broad range of social forces and the ways in which people perceived them based on cultural, religious, and socioeconomic influences. In my observation, this was one of the leading forces in accurate discovery for Beatrix; she took the time needed to view from every angle, and then she challenged and discovered new angles.

After, understanding just how Beatrix drew her conclusions, it got me thinking about the world around me, and how the masses make their assessments. The more I observed people and listened to their conversations, the more my concerns grew. My concern was for their confusion, seeing where it had led them. And then, I broadened my perspective to a wider lens of the community around me, to a variety of cultures around the globe. I could see the mound of problems, and each time I followed the trail, it led to the same answer: this can only be solved by people, with the help of other people. There are no programs that can extract the root, heal the pain, or break years of ingrained confusion. In recognizing what I learned from Beatrix—"that everyone has some of the information of truth"—I began searching for clues. I began having conversations with a wide variety of people; not a stretch, because I am fascinated by human beings and what makes them tick. The very differences dividing society became a magnet, drawing me in for a closer view. I sought to listen, observe, and understand. What I find translucent and easily detected, most others are seemingly blind to, unaware of the underlying truth.

So, how do we begin to unravel the pain and suffering of humankind that has caused such an inward attack on ourselves? I had to figure this out. Where was the tiny hidden door of opportunity, and how could I successfully step inside? I fervently prayed about how and what to do. I received much resistance from nearly every person I encountered. If not initially, it set in after going back to their camps to once again feast on fear, lies, and hatred. This was a treacherous path riddled with minefields. I kept going, and I kept talking with Beatrix to see what she might help me unfold.

After going through the proper steps of seeking permission and waiting for direction of the Higher Power, I realized that this problem was much bigger than I had imagined. I realized that my obscure life was about to become very treacherous. What could this mean for our future, the future of our children? My Higher Power, being God, just would not allow my rest or denial of this task. I attempted every excuse any person tries when avoiding the more difficult path. I finally knew that my obedience would be required, and a bigger faith than I had ever known. So, how do you convince someone to view from a different perspective? How can you get another to entertain an opposing idea to the ones they hold sacred as truth? The many conversations I had with Beatrix helped me in overcoming this hurdle. Beatrix had lived her life in a sea of contradictions, which required that she be in a constant state of discernment. Her lack of accurate discernment would have equated to harm. She knew what it meant to fly without a net over shark-infested waters. She learned quite young that she needed something, or someone, to rely on. It was very difficult, especially in her youth, to separate reality from falsehood. As children, we innately want to believe in those we love most and those whom we should be able to trust to care for us. However, Beatrix learned more about distrust and hurt. She lived in a sink-or-swim mentality. She learned to survive and accurately read her surroundings and the people within them. It forced her to go to a Higher Power for answers and guidance.

As Beatrix described her survival methods, it was easy to understand how she had developed such keen observation and discernment. She had disciplined herself to systems with evidenced proof of the success of her methods.

We all have something of great importance to offer to others. When we seek to do our very best at that task, all of humankind reaps benefits. Beatrix saw this as a responsibility, believing in serving her small purpose on earth. She never aligned her disciplines or actions to match those of society, and this often led to much misunderstanding and persecution. But Beatrix pressed on anyway, against the grain of society, pursuing purposeful living, but so very quietly. If Beatrix had been able to succeed time and again, enduring suffering for purpose, how could I not let go of excuses? After all that I had learned from Beatrix, I was—and still am—now somehow different. No, I am not really a different person; instead, I am operating in alignment to my design, my purpose. Beatrix did not change me. Rather, her characteristics, purposeful living, and authenticity to cause moved me to a different place. A better place. So, after a period of information gathering, I decided to broaden my scope through Facebook. I wondered what knowledge I might draw from a worldwide platform. It revealed more-valuable information that I could have ever imagined.

I began thinking, What are the things that influence the thoughts of people, in subtle unnoticed presentations, but then yield powerful mind-altering changes in both thought and behaviors? It is frightening to see just how easily people can be swayed in a direction. I found that this topic runs from the superficial topic of beauty, to the inner spiritual beliefs of man.

The topic of beauty and fashion begins upon birth and holds a strong influence on each gender and race. It changes decisions made, altering and tainting authentic self. I am in no way villainizing the fashion and beauty industry, as I love fashion and beautiful things. I would like to use the power this industry holds as an example of just how easily our minds take on information. This can shift quickly, as fashion often does, and we have no trouble at all keeping up with these trends. However, our minds are not as willing to accept information or trends that seem to include unwanted ideas, change, or danger for us. The greater number of people would prefer to ignore those facts and even manipulate them to whatever's needed to hold on to dysfunction. In the mind-altering world of fashion and beauty, as the trends transition and morph into new things, we are willing, even eager, to leave old trends behind as useless. What does this mean regarding the possibilities of our mind's way of forming new solutions? Does it mean that what people believed before was wrong and that the transition had brought them to a more truthful state of being? And then, when you talk to different generational age groups, you will find varying ideas of the same trend. So, what does this mean? Let's look at the more superficial topic of beauty and fashion, its powerful impact on the mind, and then the decision-making and approach afterwards. This becomes a great starting point because it impacts all of humankind. Let's review a brief history and see what conclusions we draw as to present-day thinking and approaches to daily tasks and problems needing solutions.

Beauty and Fashion Trends That Killed People

The Renaissance Era: From the 1300s well into the 1500s, this was a time in which people had a different view on beauty than most eras following it. According to much of the artwork of the era, women who had extra fat and wider hips were considered the most beautiful. In most of the paintings from the era, fuller-figured women were shown in settings where they were courted by dashing and handsome men.

The Victorian Era: From the mid-1800s through the remainder of the century, this era featured a complete reversal of beauty in body-type standards of the Renaissance period. In the Victorian era, slim waists were all the rage, to the point where it became a danger. It was a contest to have the smallest waistline, with clothing that could help women reduce their waist down to twelve inches. The clothes were constricting to the point where breathing was a chore, injuring some women with broken ribs.

The Crinoline: A hoop skirt that women in the nineteenth century wore under their actual skirts. It was made from horsehair and thread or steel. The purpose was to make the skirt look fuller. There are tales of women on piers who were swept up and carried out to sea, where they drowned because of having a steel cage tied to their waists. There were stories of skirts getting entangled in the spokes of carriages and dragging the women down the street. The poet Henry Wadsworth Longfellow's second wife went up in flames after knocking over a lit candle. In 1863, in Santiago, Chile, between two and three thousand people died in a church fire. A gas lamp lit the veils on the walls. People attempted to run outside; however, the women's skirts blocked the door. The crinolines with women inside piled up in front of the exit, making an escape impossible, even for the people who'd been smart enough not to wear hoop skirts.

The Corset: Meant to suck in a woman's "problem areas," this contraption had the small side effect of cutting off all circulation between the legs and head. With their livers in their throats and their lungs in their bellies, Victorian women invented the more voluptuous body trend. Breathing the wrong way in one of these things could break a rib, cramming the organs inward and causing internal bleeding. In 1903, a woman suffered fatal injury because of pieces of corset steel that became lodged internally. These trends in style went against the religious views of the time and were said to be works of evil.

Foot Binding: A custom for women in China, from around the eighth century until the beginning of the 1900s, this began with one concubine dancing around in front of the emperor, with silk wrapped around her feet. It became a fashion trend, and women's feet became so disfigured, they could only walk very short distances. To transform the foot from regular shaped to disfigured, women started early, at two to seven years old, when their feet were soft and their minds blissfully unaware of what would happen to their feet. First, their feet would soak in a bath that could be anything from herbs and water to urine and vinegar, depending on the family tradition. Then, all their toes except the big one were folded down, and the arch of the foot bent back. The process would go on for a few years, with ever tighter bandages and recurrently disgusting foot baths, until the feet were about three inches long. Foot binding cut off circulation in the toes, and the procedure oftentimes lead to gangrene or other life-threatening infections. A woman with normal-sized feet was considered ugly and unwedable.

Makeup: Before the age of the big-name cosmetics brands, people would smear their entire face with lead. The makeup choice of people from ancient Greece, all the way up to the 1920s in America, was a lead-based powder or lotion that rendered their faces white and became toxic to the bloodstream.

The symptoms of lead poisoning were many, including brain damage, wrecking the nervous system, headaches, loss of appetite, anemia, a constant metallic taste in the mouth, paralysis, insomnia, and, oddly enough, a limp wrist. Both men and women wore lead makeup, and as a result their faces gradually became more and more damaged. Of course, the solution to that was to cover the damage with more lead makeup!

Makeup played a huge part in helping women recover from the horrors of World War I. Before the 1920s, in America, makeup styles were seen as low class, but everything changed during Prohibition, when everyone seemingly came together in stylized fashion to find illegal ways to drink together.

The Stiff High Collar: This refers to the specific kind of high detachable collar that was especially popular in the nineteenth century. This detachable collar was a quiet assassin. By cutting off circulation, it could creep up on a man in his drunken sleep and choke him when the man's head fell forward. It could also cause asphyxia and an abscess on the brain just by being tight; or, in cases of indigestion that lead to the neck swelling, it would simply strangle its prey. One very unlucky man at the end of the 1800s was almost guillotined by his collar when he tripped coming out of a streetcar.

It may be difficult to believe that these delusional and dangerous fashion trends were accepted by everyone who was anyone at the time. What people of the times viewed in a certain way became truthful enough for them to accept the risk with no questions asked. Seriously, it seems a bit like natural selection is at work here. Could we be facing a similar problem in our thoughts and approach today, keeping us from the solutions that we are in desperate need of? You probably were a bit amused as you read through a few strange trends in history; however, don't laugh too quickly. Take a few minutes and consider similarities in our culture today. Can you see any parallels? Are we actively living out a natural selection process in society today that will be referred to as temporary insanity later? Why do we insist on disregarding truth and authenticity, in favor of the deception of passing trends and false information, all built on the flimsiness of emotion, pride, and ego? We can still enjoy beauty, fashion, and pleasure while maintaining a view of truth and making decisions based upon reality rather than fantasy. We don't have to swallow the whole pie; perhaps we can just eat a piece of pie.

> All things are lawful for me, but not all things are helpful. All things are lawful for me, but I will not be enslaved by anything.
> —1 Corinthians 6:12 (ESVUK)

We have become inundated with attaching our thoughts to all that gives us pleasure, or ranking position, but denying certain truths that are not in accord with our greed and desires. We go even further, by labeling as negative and even evil those who are able to see the truth and choose to live more wisely and balanced. In general, the trends we are most impacted by are beauty, fashion, and religion. So, how deep do these seemingly harmless designs of man impact our thoughts and actions, even making us radical and destructive to ourselves and others? Let's look at forecasted data about the more serious topic of how religion is trending. This data is such a clue for us in assessing the future, and then making our decisions to approach with wisdom and guard the preservation of man. Progression happens regardless of the thoughts one holds. This is the wiser position of determining the future in advance, and then being proactive in our decisions, for the greater good of all. Keep in mind that religion is a completely different animal than of spirituality or faith. Religion can be positive or negative, all depending on what it packages. Conversely, spirituality and faith are generally based on foundational truths provided by a power greater than humankind, and remain unchanged throughout history. Since religion holds such tremendous power in our world, it is worthwhile to have a better understanding of its forecast and what conclusions and solutions it may lead us to in our ever-meshing world.

In looking at this data, think about what is currently going on around the world, but do so in a deeper and more meaningful way. Historically, religion can be found in most conflict and seems to blind the eyes of humankind. This is not to say that religion is bad; the point is more that we may benefit from careful review of our own ideas and their roots. We must regard maintaining a peaceful existence, and honoring our differences, as more important than disagreement and destruction. So, in that state of mind, I would like for you to think, not just of yourself but of your children and grandchildren, and the world they will be left to deal with and survive in. The decisions we are making now will have impact on their quality of life. So, think back to our earlier discussion of "this" and "that" thinking. But to narrow the broader topic to a more singular thought, Do you believe their lives will hold the same borders as we know today? Is the "this" we are doing today effective for the future "that" we feel comfortable leaving our loved ones behind to survive? As you read over this data, keep yourself in reality-thinking mode, not what you wish for, have grown accustomed to, or were taught. Progression happens, regardless of an altered reality that we grasp tight within our fists.

Religious Trends

This study uses data from 198 countries and territories, on fertility, age composition, and life expectancy. It also looks at rates of changing religious affiliation (where data was available) and migration between countries, and puts all of these factors together to provide the best estimates for the future:

1. Muslims are the fastest-growing major religious group, largely because they have the highest fertility rate and the youngest population. As a result, the Muslim population is expected to increase from 1.6 billion people (23 percent

of the world's population, as of 2010) to 2.76 billion people (30 percent of all people by 2050). At midcentury, Muslims will nearly equal Christians (the world's largest religious group) in size.

Projected Change in Global Population

With the exception of Buddhists, all of the major religious groups are expected to increase in number by 2050. But some will not keep pace with global population growth, and, as a result, are expected to make up a smaller percentage of the world's population in 2050 than they did in 2010.

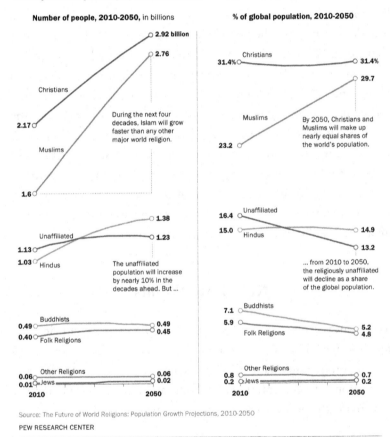

Source: The Future of World Religions: Population Growth Projections, 2010-2050

PEW RESEARCH CENTER

2. The share of the world's population that is Christian is expected to remain steady (at about 31 percent), but the regional distribution of Christians is forecast to change

significantly. Nearly four-in-ten Christians (38 percent) are projected to live in sub-Saharan Africa in 2050, an increase from the 24 percent who lived there in 2010. And the percentage of the world's Christians living in Europe—which fell from 66 percent in 1910 to 26 percent in 2010—will continue to decline, to roughly 16 percent in 2050.

3. The number of religiously unaffiliated people, also known as religious "nones," is increasing in such places as the United States and Europe, and we project continued growth. Globally, however, the opposite is true: The unaffiliated are expected to decrease as a share of the world's population between 2010 and 2050 (from 16 to 13 percent). This is attributable mostly to the relatively old age and low fertility rates of large populations of religious nones in Asian countries, particularly China and Japan.

Size and Projected Growth of Major Religious Groups

	2010 POPULATION	% OF WORLD POPULATION IN 2010	PROJECTED 2050 POPULATION	% OF WORLD POPULATION IN 2050	POPULATION GROWTH 2010-2050
Christians	2,168,330,000	31.4%	2,918,070,000	31.4%	749,740,000
Muslims	1,599,700,000	23.2	2,761,480,000	29.7	1,161,780,000
Unaffiliated	1,131,150,000	16.4	1,230,340,000	13.2	99,190,000
Hindus	1,032,210,000	15.0	1,384,360,000	14.9	352,140,000
Buddhists	487,760,000	7.1	486,270,000	5.2	-1,490,000
Folk Religions	404,690,000	5.9	449,140,000	4.8	44,450,000
Other Religions	58,150,000	0.8	61,450,000	0.7	3,300,000
Jews	13,860,000	0.2	16,090,000	0.2	2,230,000
World total	**6,895,850,000**	**100.0**	**9,307,190,000**	**100.0**	**2,411,340,000**

Source: The Future of World Religions: Population Growth Projections, 2010-2050
PEW RESEARCH CENTER

4. In the United States, Christians will decline from more than three-quarters of the population in 2010 to two-thirds in 2050, with corresponding rises of religious nones, as well as Muslims, Hindus, and others. At midcentury, Judaism will no longer be the largest non-Christian religion in the

US: Muslims are projected to be more numerous than people who identify as Jewish on the basis of religion.

5. Buddhists, concentrated in Asia, are expected to have a stable population (of just under 500 million) while other religious groups are projected to grow. As a result, Buddhists will decline as a share of the world's population (from 7 percent in 2010 to 5 percent in 2050).

6. Indonesia is currently home to the world's largest Muslim population, but that is expected to change. By 2050, the study projects India to be the country with the largest number of Muslims—more than 310 million—even though Hindus will continue to make up a solid majority of India's population (77 percent), while Muslims remain a minority (18 percent). Indonesia will have the third-largest number of Muslims, with Pakistan ranking second.

7. The farther into the future we look, the more uncertainty exists, which is why the projections stop at 2050. But if they are extended into the second half of this century, the projections forecast Muslims and Christians to be roughly equal in number around 2070, with Muslims the slightly larger group after that year.

Times of Choosing

So, why do we detach from the truth, choosing paths that lead us to destinations that we hate upon arrival? What are we thinking, when faced with decisions, big or small, making us prefer one path to another? Imagine, for a moment, two strings with objects tied to one end, and a person holding the other end. The strings are slowly being pulled down two different paths, but you do not know where the paths lead, they are just saying, "Come on, this way! Come on, this way!" On the first string, you see carefully tied images of money: a beautiful home, prestige, a nice car, extravagant vacations to your favorite places, abundant food, and lots of friends to enjoy the bounty. The person holding the string is quite good-looking. Well dressed, and with words slipping like butter from a smooth tongue, so tantalizing, so beautiful! This person has it all and so surely knows the path to choose. Behold! You can't even take your eyes off this stunning individual. You're thinking, *It's my lucky day; my ship has come in!* You look behind you to make sure no one will follow your footsteps, because this treasure is meant for you alone. You have worked hard, and you deserve it! *What about my family?* you wonder but then quickly reassure yourself, *Oh, they will be fine; they will adjust, when they see what I bring back to them. Man, I am the bomb!* You look around one more time, making sure the coast is clear. *Whew, no one is following me!* You begin walking, without a single question, following the tempter who offers you such opportunity. You know if you question anything, you may lose out on the treasure. You begin walking, trying to grab the end of the string, which escapes your fingers each time you attempt to grab it. But you are determined to get it. You just try harder and walk even faster. No one will take what's yours!

Meanwhile, another person has approached the other string. You didn't see this person. You think to yourself, *Hah, I saw that other string, and there wasn't even anything on it. It was leading to nowhere, and it looked like a poor vagrant was holding it.*

Both strings have disappeared into the distance, along with the persons following them (you and another), and we won't know for some time where their paths took them. This visual concept tells us much about the concepts from historical events both in beauty/fashion and religion. The two often-opposing entities drive almost every aspect of our culture, from very small unnoticed daily routines, to our biggest life-changing moments. The historical data showed us some crazy and even amusing things that people just swallowed without question, getting on board as quickly as possible. It also revealed some trends currently under way that most haven't a clue are happening. None of the information, standing alone, is a bad thing. Information is just that: information. The relevant point is how we choose to act, or not act, upon the information in question. We are the sources responsible for how information impacts our lives. What does this mean about our past and our daily choices now? Do you believe the people in history were somehow less informed than we are today? Or, was it that very little thought went into the choices being made? Could they also have been emotionally connecting to the items of temptation? Did their emotions and ego take over, leading them to choose to follow lust, greed, selfishness, or fitting in? Were they just willingly accepting deception, without question?

Exercise

After reviewing the forecast for religion and keeping in mind the current societal viewpoints (the way in which people are seeing things and events, and then responding), create a two-sided snapshot visual of future outcomes:

1. The first one should be as you see it being played out today. Honestly answer this question for yourself: Where does the current trajectory of our path end as a destination for humankind? Consider carefully, and then support ideas with data and your own opinions drawn from a state of truth. Do not allow smoke and mirrors, or fluff-and-stuff thinking. (Apply the tools you have acquired to assist you with outcomes.)

2. Create a second future outcome based on what you believe a better destination might be. You must support your idea with an actionable plan of the things needed to change trajectory. How can you implement them strategically for success? You must calculate for both dangers and risks.

Then, attach your plan to humankind and describe what adjustments will be needed from the human-capital standpoint in order to reach a more desirable destination.

Root Extractor

Lord, I know that people's lives are not their own; it is not for them to direct their steps.

—Jeremiah 10:23 (NIV)

It is not in the power of humans to determine what will happen to them. Human ideas have finite wisdom and ability, and this has limited human understanding of truth. If we couple this with the corrupt sinfulness of human nature, we understand that humans simply cannot direct their own steps. What seems right to humanity results in the path of destruction and death. As human thoughts are not God's, so must human ways likewise fall short of God's perfect and all-wise plan.

Discovering the root of pain or problems is imperative to solutions that will provide lasting change. How does one get to the root of the matter? This is most often where people get lazy with details and facts. They cry for change, yet they take the easy way out. They say they believe one thing, yet they act out the opposite. They become so committed to the rules of whatever or whomever they follow that truth disappears completely into the background. They soon begin to act against the very beliefs they claimed as guiding lights. This brings societal rules back into the spotlight again, which conflicts with truth. I am in no way attempting to sway your personal beliefs or faith. Each of us must make this decision for ourselves. However, for the integrity of the events that I'll describe, it's important that I should disclose my own underlying beliefs. It's important to disclose what we believe so that we may understand one another better. Not for agreement's sake but for understanding so that we can weigh it properly with our own belief systems. I want a clear understanding of where my personal rules and tools are rooted. Oftentimes, the things that reveal what we need to know for solutions are unknown to us and may even feel wrong. We are certain to find failure by relying on our own ideas alone. Our own ideas and minds are limited, making no amount of education able to bring us closer to the deep-rooted issues of society or individual circumstances. Throughout my own investigative studies and the many hours of discussions with Beatrix, I found we shared similar experiences. Once you begin asking questions, people tend to clam up. This is a hindrance to what people profess wanting, in turn becoming a hindrance to resolving the problems we face. I experienced the false accusations of having ill motives, just as Beatrix experienced. She even experienced an accusation of being a witch. Yes, you read that correctly: she was accused of being a witch because of her God-given ability to accurately predict outcomes and act in advance of them. These were particularly discouraging and dangerous times. When you are assessing the losses and dangers for the sake of others, the very ones you advocate for often turn on you or throw you under the bus. They have become so trapped in their minds as to how things have been and what they know that they panic and end up adding danger to those who could have assisted them. We must get to the root, and find the source of pain, in order for any corrective actions to have a chance at succeeding. This can only be achieved through open communication and understanding of the challenges.

Why is it so difficult to challenge our thoughts, our cultural beliefs, and even our religion? For most, this stirs a defensive response, even at the risk of not solving the problem. We tend to respond differently to physical pain because it's more tangible.

When we are sick, the symptoms of our illness usually show up before the root cause is exposed. In society, we see symptoms of paralyzing anxiety, out-of-control anger, marriages in distress, financial chaos, and many more. We lack peace and long for relief. Where did this pain originate? Our Great Physician offers us clarity, answers, and help.

> Guard your heart above all else, for it determines
> the course of your life.
> —Proverbs 4:23 (NLT)

The condition of our heart determines the course or paths we choose. God reveals that the condition of our hearts will determine the course of our lives. What is inside your heart is taking you somewhere! Sick heart equals sick life. Healthy heart equals healthy life.

Your heart is highly valuable. We don't guard something that's worth nothing. When I take out my trash, I'm fine with walking away. As long as it's gone, I'm not too concerned with who comes and gets it. However, I would never intentionally leave something of value sitting on the street corner, or cash my paycheck and give it to my children to play store. When something is valuable, we guard it. We protect it. Your heart is of huge value. And God says to guard it! But why do we need to guard our hearts? Our hearts are under attack. Just like bacteria or disease can attack our physical bodies, there is also real assault attempting an attack of our heart. The very nature of the words "guard your heart" indicate that there is something we must guard against. The Bible is clear that we have enemies. One thing is for sure, the enemy knows with certainty the root and source of our pain. If we, as people, cannot succeed at extracting the root ourselves, it will be revealed to us as lessons we can't afford. Could we be seeing our own deeds of sickened hearts and minds beginning to play out? Have we chosen to leave God behind as something we are far too advanced to need? Can God assist people who have grown to be lovers of themselves, lusters of society, while completely disregarding Him? Do we just throw His name around for personal show, all the while lacking the substance He offers within? Some may refer to the unfolding of destruction as karma; others call it discipline from a Higher Power. Whatever you may call it, balance is always restored. We become easily fooled by the gifts of free will. We begin to use our freedom for selfish or destructive purposes. Even after our missteps, we are granted mercy and time to correct our own paths, but have our hearts hardened to where we are blinded?

We actively seek knowledge but not wisdom. Knowledge can be easily obtained from another, whereas wisdom is only acquired through our own hard work, skin in the game, and extracting what no longer serves us. Wisdom is certainly not sought after today; instead, we trade wisdom for what we can buy, work for, or inherit from another. Certainly, society has no reward for wisdom, so we prefer and choose the baited path. Where can that path possibly lead us? People want to be heard and want to have a voice, but no one listens to the voices of one another—and certainly not to the voice of God. We need for people to like us, see us, and praise us, and we feel incomplete without hero worship. Most of us would allow the voice of a friend to guide our actions, only using God as a last resort, or never at all. How can God respond to this mind-set we have chosen to root deeply by refusing to weed our own gardens? It is far too easy to point fingers of blame, fight over everything, and be perfectly satisfied with accomplishing nothing, until the next shoe drops. Then, we cycle right back through all the same thoughts and actions, never thinking that perhaps we should get off this merry-go-round. Might we consider thinking differently and seeking what we are missing? It will look strange to be the one stepping off the ride, but it may be worth the risk. When we lose our way, and we all do at times, it is part of our humanness to remain stuck. The second and most important part is discovery of the root of the problem that led us down the wrong path in the first place. This discovery requires a humble heart, a remorseful heart, and an understanding that we can no longer allow those same weeds to grow in our gardens, our hearts, or our minds. If we do not succeed at making the necessary choices for restoration, perhaps even refusing to do so, this opens the door for a more Sovereign Judge. What is sovereignty?

Sovereignty can be defined as having supreme authority, control, and power over all that has happened, is happening, and will happen in the future, in all times across all history. Believers define it as the Ruler of the Universe (God) having the right, the authority, and the power to govern all that happens. This includes what has, is, or will happen being in accordance with His divine will. He has the right to achieve His purposes and the power to bring about circumstances that dictate whatever He wills to come to pass. He has complete control of everything, and there is nothing that is done that is not done by or allowed through His will.

> It is for freedom that Christ has set us free. Stand firm, then, and do not be encumbered once more by a yoke of slavery.
>
> —Galatians 5:1 (BSB)

> Stay alert! Watch out for your great enemy, the devil. He prowls around like a roaring lion, looking for someone to devour.
>
> —1 Peter 5:8 (NLT)

> For we are not fighting against flesh-and-blood enemies, but against evil rulers and authorities of the unseen world, against mighty powers in this dark world, and against evil spirits in the heavenly places.
>
> —Ephesians 6:12 (NLT)

Chapter 6

Mojo Anger

Questions or Answers?

We become frustrated and confused by what we don't understand, or what we thought we understood that turns out to be false. We should execute caution here. As humans, when we are upset, we tend to look for someone to blame, and it usually turns out to be the wrong person or thing. We are triggered to respond in ways that usually work counter to what we really want. And then, society tells us we shouldn't be negative. Anger is a normal response to wrong actions unjustly against us. We should not act in negative or vindictive ways, even when something negative has been done against us.

There is so much mistrust fueling the fire that was already smoldering. Now we have lost trust in the very things we thought made us strong. We feel duped, and much of that may be legitimate. We are worried about the moral health of society, and this is suppressing the satisfaction of humankind. We have become discontent with the dishonesty of elected officials, and this is leading to distrust of government. In the broadest sense, these ethical concerns are now weighing down our attitudes and our ability to survive.

Disillusionment with and cynicism toward our political leaders is an important factor in distrust of government. We have lost trust in the way the government performs its duties for the citizens it is supposed to represent and support. And then, we see government officials attempting to stir strife among the people. We simply cannot go down the path of inward fighting among ourselves. This is a time for questioning the many whys of all this madness. The more we ask the correct questions, the closer we will come to solutions. This can become tricky regarding party affiliations. You may need to incorporate a no-party rule, while in active brainstorming of the questions most in need of answers. I am unaffiliated, and I have a rule of thumb that keeps me grounded. My rule is simple: never fall in love with a candidate or party; it will only serve to cloud your vision. Perhaps you begin in the confines of family and intimate friends, and then work your way into the greater community, gathering questions that need answering. Focus on the questions, not the answers. This may sound easy, but once you start down the rabbit hole, you will be very surprised at the enlightenment you stumble upon. We are near a crisis stage in every aspect of our lives. Our families are broken and troubled, our communities are riddled with crime, drugs, and danger, and it seems that the world is coming to a fast boiling-over point. Public desire for activism has risen, but it has not yet found its footing for change. The distrust of officials has fostered a disregard for the nation's laws, eroding patriotism and encouraging fighting among one another. We must take strong caution in how our feelings are impacting our daily lives, thoughts, and actions toward one another. Certainly, we should be taking time to deal with these emotions within ourselves and our families, ensuring that everyone has an escape plan in place for dealing with events and emotions we normally would not plan for. We would be remiss in not having these discussions, not based on fear but on planning and readiness. Our children are in desperate need of guidance, and because we feel this is too difficult for us, they are left to fend for themselves. It is a most critical time to bring the youth and elders together, adjoining the past and present for a better future. The manner in which we come through this time depends upon our stepping up and addressing how we will cope constructively together. Jesus Himself gave evidence to us about anger, and how to use it constructively.

Was Jesus Ever Angry?

When Jesus cleared the temple of the money changers and animal sellers, He showed great emotion and anger. (Matthew 21:12–13; Mark 11:15–18; John 2:13–22) Jesus's emotion was described as "zeal" for God's house (John 2:17). His anger was pure and completely justified because at its root was concern for God's holiness and worship. Because these were at stake, Jesus took quick and decisive action. Another time Jesus showed anger was in the synagogue of Capernaum. When the Pharisees refused to answer Jesus's questions, "He looked around at them in anger, deeply distressed at their stubborn hearts" (Mark 3:5).

Many times, we think of anger as a selfish, destructive emotion that we should eradicate from our lives altogether. However, the fact that Jesus did sometimes become angry indicates that anger itself, as an emotion, is amoral. This is borne out elsewhere in the New Testament. Ephesians 4:26 instructs us "in your anger do not sin," and not to let the sun go down on our anger. The command is not to "avoid anger" (or suppress it or ignore it) but to deal with it properly, in a timely manner. We note the following facts about Jesus's displays of anger:

1. **His anger had the proper motivation.** In other words, He was angry for the right reasons. Jesus's anger did not arise from petty arguments or personal slights against Him. There was no selfishness involved.

2. **His anger had the proper focus.** He was not angry at God or at the "weaknesses" of others. His anger targeted sinful behavior and true injustice.

3. **His anger had the proper supplement.** Mark 3:5 says that His anger was attended by grief over the Pharisees' lack of faith. Jesus's anger stemmed from love for the Pharisees and concern for their spiritual condition and lack of faith. It had nothing to do with hatred or ill will.

4. **His anger had the proper control.** Jesus was never out of control, even in His wrath. The temple leaders did not like His cleansing of the temple (Luke 19:47), but He had done nothing sinful. He controlled His emotions; His emotions did not control Him.

5. **His anger had the proper duration.** He did not allow His anger to turn into bitterness; He did not hold grudges. He dealt with each situation properly, and He handled anger in good time.

6. **His anger had the proper result.** Jesus's anger had the inevitable consequence of godly action. As with all His emotions, Jesus's anger was held in check by the Word of God; thus, Jesus's response was always to accomplish God's will.

When we get angry, we all too often have improper control or an improper focus. We fail in one or more of the above points. This is the wrath of man, of which we are told. Jesus did not exhibit human anger, but, rather, the righteous indignation of God.

> This you know, my beloved brethren. But everyone must be quick to hear, slow to speak and slow to

anger; for the anger of man does not achieve the righteousness of God. (James 1:19–20)

We must learn to harness our anger and aggression, and use them as a springboard for coming together and fueling the necessary and appropriate solutions. If we dismiss the anger, it will inevitably explode in ways that we can't afford as individuals or as a society. We have no control over the actions of others in response to the problems we are facing, but if more people take on a proactive approach, putting their anger and frustration to work, much could be accomplished. And at this point, any movement forward is better than waiting for another to fix the problems. The brewing undertone of distrust has had, and continues to have, dangerous consequences for all of humankind.

How do we get to the truth, both within our deeper selves and in our view of what's going on around us? We have talked quite a bit about assessing and understanding how to root out a matter, rather than just going with our feelings, what someone has told us, or the preferences of our individual personalities. The biggest deceptions we deal with are the ones we allow or create for a purpose. We may not be fully aware that we are doing it, or we may be blatantly aware. It may be for the purpose of survival or because of a given scenario. So, if we want to see what's going on within ourselves and the outer world, questions are the path to revealing what we need to know. Begin by questioning yourself, and really applying the methods and tools you have acquired thus far, to extract your own deep-rooted feelings, motives, and questions.

Exercise

Write down at least ten questions that you need answered. They can be personal, or they can be broader in scope.

After writing down your questions, go to a person you trust and ask for ten questions he or she would like answers to. See how this information coincides—or conflicts—and then see how this leads to your next questions.

Anger Brings Awareness

Most people are so inundated with the popular view of positive or negative thinking that they never challenge thoughts, or, in many cases, even think at all. They just fall in line with the masses around them; after all, that is the path of least resistance. And still many more practice incorrect processing of thoughts and anger. My mind naturally goes to visual places when I am sorting information. When I begin, I start with the visualization of a tabletop with mounds of information upon it (representing surface noise), and then, taking my hand and with one swoop, sending it flying to the floor, scattered as rubbish. With that image in place, we are ready to get started! You must prepare your mind for neutrally discerning truth. Completely forget the nonsense of positive and negative thinking, for they will lead you astray. By allowing yourself to think truthfully, you open yourself to the possibility for discernment of truth. As you begin to explore the details around you in a new way, you will see how truthful thinking provides accuracy, lending itself to useful and productive solutions. Removing biases, the things you've learned or were told by another, allows accurate deductive reasoning. You have thus created an unobstructed path to gaining the truth. If you discern incorrectly, you will have gathered clouded, even dishonest, information. Can you see how this will only create useless solutions? Garbage in, garbage out. We observe this happening around us every day. Seemingly smart or educated people have either no solutions at all or ridiculous solutions bound for failure. So, keep in mind that when you take on the views of others, or a negative/positive mentality, you have willingly placed blinders on your eyes, causing you to miss vital details needed in the assessments you make.

Humans possess the amazing ability to endure and survive, although it seems we may have forgotten many of our instincts. In any scenario that may put us in harm's way or jeopardy, our instincts tend to take over, attempting to create a form of protection. If you are conscious of this process, then it is not a bad thing, because you are using it as a tool. Once you have made the transition away from the situation, the tool will simply be put back into your tool belt. The key point is to be *consciously aware,* and then understand how and when to use your tools. The sad truth is that most are not conscious of this happening; instead, they just become another version of themselves that matches the tool (i.e., a "tough guy"). They basically begin to lose the authentic self, becoming the tool. This very singular approach results in a lack of full development of the self.

We can see examples of how Beatrix learned to become multifaceted, and yet maintained her authentic self. She understood her tools well, and she learned how to use them without becoming them. In contrast, her mother was not able to accomplish this, which led to her demise in many respects. It wasn't her fault that she was faced with insurmountable obstacles and dangers. Eventually, she lost her authentic self and her strength to endure any further. She slowly separated from self and reality.

This provides a valuable lesson of awareness for us as individuals, and also in regard to the problems we are facing. Will we lose ourselves among the noise and frustration, or will we rise to a greater state of effective awareness? Will we choose to change our path, and thereby secure a better future?

Look in the Mirror: See Authentic You

> For I do not understand my own actions. For I do
> not do what I want, but I do the very thing I hate.
> Now if I do what I do not want, I agree with the law,
> that it is good. So now it is no longer I who do it, but
> sin that dwells within me. For I know that nothing
> good dwells in me, that is, in my flesh. For I have
> the desire to do what is right, but not the ability to
> carry it out. For I do not do the good I want, but the
> evil I do not want is what I keep on doing.
>
> —Romans 7:15–24 (ESV)

This is a most difficult process for all people, yet it should be a daily routine of checking the self in relation to your position in the world around you. It is tough for any of us to look in the mirror and embrace our true self, in part because of all the conflicting information we have received up to this point. Some of us know we have been drastically misunderstood and underestimated, and yet no spoken words would ever convince those around us to view us differently. And then, there are others who have been defined to be more than they are capable of being, and the system around them offers enough protection and comfort so that there is no advantage of revealing the true self. At this moment, depending on your age, cultural roots, family of origin, gender, race, and even religious beliefs, your ideas of yourself may be very altered, even untrue. Since childhood, you have been receiving labels and placed in boxes of confinement and control. You may be telling yourself it isn't so, but, trust me, it is. We even take on a facade for ourselves to protect the more vulnerable authentic self underneath. There are times when this can be wise and strategically beneficial. However, this can become problematical when you begin to believe the labels others have placed upon you to be truth. You will begin acting out their definition of you or shutting down your true self completely.

This can be a tough truth to face, but it is also the route to freedom and the solutions you desperately need. You will never find the guiding light and balancer for yourself while living out a facade. And this is no simple mishap. It will impact every aspect of your existence: the person you marry, the career you choose, the friends you surround yourself with, and your overall success in life. It will impact generations after you, if not corrected. It is impossible to unlock your mind to new ways of thought process and approach when you aren't operating in an authentic mode. So, it is necessary to understand oneself in relation to the world, in order to access new information for conquering the hauntings of the past and/or whatever life may throw at you in the present.

Beatrix knew herself well. I believe that to be one of the most important reasons that she was able to endure so much, remain intact, and not give in to the weakness of those around her. She always chose to rise above, even when she was terribly hurt and angry.

Beatrix on Knowing Yourself

You must know yourself! If you don't know yourself first, you will never know another. When you need to make moves to either advocate for others or effect necessary changes, you will not be able to stand firm if you don't know and understand yourself well.

For most of my career, I was in some form of sales. The first sales job I took, I was in my early twenties. The company I worked for had all sales staff do both personality and communication profiles. This gave the employer insights as to how to get the best from us, the employees. It also gave the employees insights as to how to create our interactions with potential customers. This was such a turning point in my personal development. When I took this sales job, I had one purpose: to make enough money to be able to stay at home with my first child. I was very shy and lacked confidence at the time, but I was motivated by my daughter. Each family member that I told about my new venture laughed out loud at my attempt. It was discouraging, but I was plugged into my goal of not having my daughter in day care, so I ignored them. Understand, I was always the quiet one in the room, very happy just blending into the background. I can see why it might have seemed strange that I would take on such a venture. But it was the single most-important step in learning more about who I really was. I had been convinced by others' opinions that my opportunities were limited. But my first child gave me just enough willpower to overcome my fears.

This may seem simple, but, for Beatrix, it became a real turning point. She knew that what she heard about herself, what kept echoing around her in relation to who she was, wasn't quite true. But she also wasn't sure what was actually true about her. Maybe they were right. She tried, but no one would listen to her. She learned to exist and keep her thoughts within her. For the most, part her family discouraged her with words of harsh criticism and false descriptions. Beatrix went on to explain that, initially, she didn't fully understand the meaning of the profiles, but they did at least affirm that she wasn't the negative words that had been used to describe her. When completing the profiles, she was able to answer honestly from within, and no one could stop that truth. It gave her hope in what she knew about herself, and she could use this small confirmation to begin believing in her authentic self. Beatrix had a most unusual personality type: an INTJ, and female. The INTJ personality type is one of the rarest, especially among women. Women of this personality type are especially rare, forming just 0.8% of the entire population. Being so rare, other people may have a difficult time understanding an INTJ. I share this with you so that you will have a better perspective of why she operated in unusual ways that always seemed to bring misunderstanding of her. This was especially difficult for her as a young girl growing up in the southern United States, as women had been narrowly defined. Beatrix knew she was different, but she had been taught it was wrong—that she was wrong simply for being herself. It made her life very difficult and lonely. She learned to adapt to becoming unseen and unheard; she learned to just be what her family and community needed her to be. At the time of her childhood, this was a region where women very much had, and knew, their place, and it was a very quiet and submissive place.

That said, profiles such as the ones Beatrix referred to, should be kept in proper perspective, as an aid or a tool, not a self-definition. They can help you gain meaningful understanding of the world around you. But you must keep in mind the sliding scale that is different for all, depending on other influences. If you have never done such a process for yourself, you can access many of the standard tests on the internet, one being the Myers-Briggs Type Indicator (MBTI). You can do simple tests or in-depth studies. I will leave this to your discretion, as, again, such a test is merely a tool, not a foundational truth.

> Let no one deceive himself. If any of you thinks he is wise in this age, he should become a fool, so that he may become wise.
> —1 Corinthians 3:18 (ESV)

> Do you see a man who is wise in his own eyes? There is more hope for a fool than for him.
> —Proverbs 26:12 (ESV)

Understanding Others

> But as for the highly esteemed, whatever they were makes no difference to me; God does not show

favoritism. For those leaders added nothing to my
message.

—Galatians 2:6 (BSB)

For if a man think himself to be something, when
he is nothing, he deceives himself.

—Galatians 6:3 (NIV)

"Believe half of what you say, a third of what you see, and none
of what you hear." This is an adage that comes from a place of
wisdom. It will allow you to build bridges, rather than blowing
them up, usually while people are on them. Don't fall for the trap
of judging people incorrectly as a result of what appears to be or
what you may have heard. Don't listen to gossip, and don't initiate
gossip. Rumors and speculations run rampant at every turn, and
even by merely listening, we are as guilty as the one spreading the
misnomers. This works just the same as every other concept we
have covered so far: you must do the work yourself.

People are the energy source from which things happen. Humans
embody the power behind creation and destruction, so it is
imperative to understand those you encounter. Discipline yourself
to use methods of forming your own opinions. So, how you will
detect if you are mastering this skill? It is simple: if you have
mastered this skill, no one will ever come to you with gossip. I can
attest to this personally. No one who knows me ever comes to me
with gossip. Why? Because I stop it cold. Once this is learned or
known about you, no one will ever come to you with gossip again.
Gossiping is both an immature and irresponsible action, and it only
leads to hurting others. If we wish to demonstrate having correct
motives, we must avoid this pitfall and do the work necessary to
understand those around us. The greatest gift you can ever give a
person is to truly know him or her. This takes time, good motives,
and a broader mind, all of which are necessary to receive the other

person in his or her authentic form, discounting any preconceived notions you might have.

> Where no wood is, [there] the fire goeth out: so where [there is] no talebearer, the strife ceaseth.
> —Proverbs 26:20 (KJV)

> He who goes about as a talebearer reveals secrets,
> But he who is trustworthy conceals a matter.
> —Proverbs 11:13 (NASB)

As you know, Beatrix began her career in sales. She became very successful, earning numerous awards and incentive trips, and this led to her eventually owning her own business. She shared techniques that she used when training her sales staff. As Beatrix explained to me, it was never difficult to train employees in the function of job performance, but it was very difficult to train them in the basics of understanding people. She herself was a natural at this, much like a natural athlete. Her ability was *concise understanding* of the people around her. She emphasized the importance of two basic components of understanding others: (1) "it's not about me," and (2) decide each person's "flavor" within the first ten seconds of meeting him or her. A partial list of components appears below.

Beatrix on Understanding Others

1. **It is not about you.** You are part of the equation, as related to the responses of others, so, table your emotions completely. Table your ideas completely. Be a *neutral* slate in terms of both decision and method.
2. **Quickly determine the person's flavor.** You have only a few seconds in any scenario to decide who you are dealing with. This ability will take practice, but it will give you

much-needed insights in terms of making the correct approach to that person.

3. **Accurately assess the person's strengths and weaknesses.** Locating the best entry point will be key to successful outcomes. "Back door" entry is optimal. Unassuming and unnoticed entry is key to success.

4. **Approach all people on their individual level and meet them on their turf.** Adjust yourself to meet each person eye to eye. Do not attempt to pull anyone to your ground.

The Ice-Cream Theory

How does ice cream relate to understanding or problem solving in human interactions? Here, Beatrix expands on the concept of each person's flavor.

Beatrix

This is where I apply what I refer to as the *ice-cream theory,* a simple method I used to teach employees who struggled with understanding others. This approach helps keep you on track by staying fully focused on the needs and desires of the other person. I also call this determining the person's *flavor.* Upon meeting the person, be mentally aware of what flavor ice cream he or she prefers, based on his or her personality type. When you first encounter a person, you have a few seconds to determine the best approach for the desired outcome. Meaning, the best approach to *uncovering* the real need of the person, or what he or she is looking to gain. Oftentimes, this is different from, or even opposite of, what the person tells you. Most people will tell you what they were told to say or believe. If you have not prepared for each step of approach, this is where it will begin to show up, and opportunity will be lost. And, remember, you may only get one shot.

So, in a matter of seconds, you will learn how to decide which flavor ice cream the person "needs" in your delivery to them. What flavor does the person like? Do not try to serve your favorite flavor to the person; that will be disastrous. Remember, the person does not care what your favorite flavor is, so you must sideline yourself. Check your ego and emotions completely! Before trying this, maybe have a very simple ice-cream code key developed for yourself. You can tweak and reinvent it as you become more comfortable with it. Perhaps vanilla is your very low-key, quiet people; strawberry might be your fun-loving people; chocolate could be your strong-willed, full-tilt people. I use a more complex process; however, a very simple model needs to be attempted if this is not a normal process for your own personality. Mirror the person. People love to see their reflection in others; it gives them comfort and builds bridges. Now, don't stay too long on this process the first few times you try it. What I mean is, if you have never approached people/ scenarios like this before, it needs to be just a quick assessment, and then remove yourself from the situation. If not, it will become very awkward, very fast. They will sense a negative feeling, and it will work against everything. This is more for you to gather information and then remove yourself to review what you have learned. And then you can begin to test your theories and become an expert at handling scenarios with people in order to achieve results. The most important thing to remember is: *This is not about you!* This is about how you respond in a different and more positive way to get the desired results. Your goal should be helping others get what they need and want. By serving the needs of others first, your needs will also be furnished. Never the reverse order! For the most part, your needs are irrelevant. Always work with people with correctly aligned motives, and always put them first.

By seeking to understand the need of others first, your spiritual awareness becomes awakened, aligning to your ability to help others on a larger scale. Beatrix lived and breathed this concept in all she pursued. She understood her purpose of serving, and she used her ability to understand people for the greater good of those she loved and served.

Assumptions Are Rarely True

Assumptions are unsubstantiated ideas or biases; they are not the same as truth. We see this evidenced daily, threatening the fabric of our families and communities, and the larger world. This was an obstacle that Beatrix had to overcome constantly. However, she learned how to take the bullets aimed at her and use that as another tool to conquer opposition. She could have given up; instead, she made it into a game. She would chuckle and say, "I can use your bullet in my gun!" This kept her in a more positive spirit for the challenges she faced. It became a bit of a chess match to her. She could have chosen to treat them equally badly, but she knew that would only make her just like the ones who were acting unfairly against her or others. Joining that team was a despicable thought to Beatrix. So, she had to learn ways to absorb the heat, take their punches, and then move right past them, toward whatever her goal happened to be.

Beatrix on Assumptions

It was so difficult to take all the nasty and illegitimate assumptions others were making about me. I tried a few times to overcome their ideas, to no avail. Since quitting was never an option, and neither was convincing them otherwise, I learned to use it as yet another tool in my belt. It was terribly frustrating and very hurtful, but I did not allow it to change my course or the integrity of how I treated others. There were those who were so cruel and hurtful that, over time, I decided that avoidance was best. There was no practical benefit for remaining. It was difficult at times, working for people who treated me with utter disrespect, and yet sucking it up, just to get the job done. I did not fail them, even when they hurt or abused me. In business, I made it a challenge for myself, and it was a bit easier to reconcile the lack of regard of emotion. Because emotion in business is a no-no. So, I learned to use it as a tool in overcoming obstacles, staying clear of trip wires, and checkmating the enemy. This eventually aided in my excelling right past the nasty, assuming labelers. Assumptions lead to false labeling of people, placing them in tidy little boxes, then becoming their definition of truth in both family and society. Assumptions become a heinous enemy to truth and have even led to the murdering of innocents throughout history. And if they aren't murdered physically, they were still murdered by the tongue. This affects all aspects of the quality of their lives; many of them face ostracism in their own families and communities, making their lives unbearably miserable. The pack mentality sets in, and there are simply too many minds to change. Victims become outnumbered, so they must find ways to survive the environment. By this time, the assumptive lies have taken the form of truth, and they continue to manifest into new, different, and worse versions each time they are spoken. But it goes even further, affecting the jobs they will be able to obtain and having a decided impact on their income. No amount of letting people get to know you can change this dynamic. So, as the assuming labelers go about their lives, able to apply their energy to productive works to advance themselves and their families, their victims spend most of their energy just fighting the dynamics that set a fire in their lives, trying to beat out the flames. The more they try, the more it fuels the fire. Their efforts and energies are gobbled up in worthless attempts, leaving them to just spin their wheels but never gain traction or momentum.

As I listen and watch people advocating for the rights of race, gender, or religion, and see them repeating the same failed efforts repeatedly, I want to just scream, "Stop! That's not going to work!"

The unfortunate truth of the matter is that if you attempt to explain this to them, they would turn their frustration on you instead. There are rare occasions when you can adjust the thoughts of humankind. Typically, it is when they are feeling great loss, and even then, you will only be able to reach the wiser ones. So, I just watch in dismay and frustration. It is like watching people stand on a train track, with on oncoming train fast approaching. You just stand there in terror, watching, and you try to coax the ones who are unaware, get them to move off the train track to safety. They look at you in confusion, somehow believing you are the bad guy. This becomes maddening in the mind. It also shows just how powerful assumptions are in defining truth to people. They hold on to the very thing that is about to destroy them, while believing truth to be the lie. This became the most difficult thing to keep reconciling within myself: working honestly on the behalf of others in ways they could not accomplish, most too blind to even see. No appreciation, and oftentimes a swift kick in the face, for your hard work and honest efforts to help them. *Really? Why do I even bother?* How can you care for others, and be cared for so little? I could never understand this. It always hurt deeply, but I stayed true to them, once again "casting my pearls before swine." But, I did get wiser in the attempts I made, and with whom. It was difficult, but you can't help those who refuse your assistance, no matter how good your intentions might be.

> "Do not give what is holy to the dogs; nor cast your
> pearls before swine, lest they trample them under
> their feet, and turn and tear you in pieces."
> —Matthew 7:6 (KJV)

Beatrix on Overcoming

So, even when you discover the window of opportunity, to finally overcome the ill-fated assumptions, your next pressing factor becomes timing and method of delivery. You must work quietly and unnoticed. You do this by simply becoming the label assigned to you. You focus on the mission, the goal, and then you detach from their ignorance. However, use their ignorance as a tool in the mission! The moment you engage with them otherwise, perhaps the way in which you prefer, you will be trampled. This is a discipline of submission on behalf of the cause. You must focus on the goal, the mark of destination. You already know you are dealing with confused people; they have certainly mislabeled you and don't even understand themselves. So, you must maintain this truthful understanding of the minds of the people you are dealing with. Confused people become dangerous for you, others, and the goal. Never underestimate the problems or dangers that ignorance can set off. You must work with extreme caution.

If you just blow in on people, spilling your observations or awareness, they will not just calmly say, "Oh, okay. Thank you." It disturbs them greatly and makes them angry; they may even turn against you, when you are only there to help. I have found only one method to safely deliver controversial information: one that people cannot see, or fear. I have tested other methods, and the results were never as desired. So, I learned to exercise patience and find delivery methods that would result in the efforts needed for success.

It required accessing a different power, a reliable power that would help me move beyond myself, entailing both my strengths and weaknesses as effective tools against the opposition. Otherwise, I would have to be satisfied living out the life the labeler assigned to me and others. I knew that all their assumptions were incorrect, but there is no way to explain your way out of an assumption that has been assigned you. Every interaction with those around you becomes tainted with the assumptions assigned to you. There is no easy way to overcome an assumption that has been assigned. If you speak up, they use your words to further embellish lies against you.

I tried all logical and reasonable attempts of societal standards and accepted norms, only to be shoved deeper into a bigger hole. What to do? What possible options are left for effective existence and survival? I had exhausted all ideas of my own understanding. And then, in a prayerful moment, God spoke to me, instructing me on a new approach. So often I had heard or read the verse containing these words: "Lean not on your own understanding." What does that even mean? I only learned the meaning through obedience. Sometimes it seems that we pray forever, with no answer from God. But desiring to do good, I continued to pray, sometimes with much frustration, almost ready to throw in the towel. But He finally answered, and I am certain that the answer could not have come before my own readiness to receive it. God is always right on time, not a moment too early or too late. He instructed me to stop my own actions, my conversations, or my attempts to reason with the assuming labelers. Instead, I was to stand still and allow the assuming labelers to do whatever they pleased, taking no action against them, allowing them to fully show themselves, with no resistance. My only instructions were to "stand still, do nothing, and allow them to reveal exactly who they are, and then, this time, to believe them." To understand this divine instruction more fully, you need to understand that a strength of mine (awareness) was being transformed into a huge weakness. It seemed that through this door of weakness, the plots of those who meant harm to me and those I loved had room to design and execute their malignant intentions freely. But I agreed to the terms, and it was most difficult to execute, as I will further describe in all that followed. The main idea to carry forward in this discovery is that I was forced to just be an onlooker and not even defend myself against false information. I was always proactive, but something different was now required of me. At the time, this instruction just did not make any sense to me. It seemed completely illogical; however, it proved to be exactly the correct process to deliver me and those I loved from adversarial hands. And this time, the stakes were much higher than I had ever known. This time, I was at the hands of very dangerous and powerful people. This time, the stakes were high; even, perhaps, my own life. But what was on the line was so much more important.

> Trust in the LORD with all your heart and lean not
> on your own understanding; in all your ways submit
> to him, and he will make your paths straight.
> —Proverbs 3:5–6 (NIV)

After what I discovered, I had no choice but to step forward. I had to make sure these skills were revealed to help people, even if they became initially upset. I knew the challenge would be much bigger than I was, far greater than my capabilities. I had to teach these methods. I had no idea if my own methods would have worked in this situation. I had only the instructions from God "to go"! I had no idea what would happen, and just enough faith and obedience to start walking. Just me and God. I was sure it would be the end for me, but the deal had been struck. There was no turning back.

When it began to succeed, I was in awe! The methods I had practiced for so many years (given to me by God) had endured a most extreme test. The methods I had safely practiced for years had helped me communicate and exist undetected among killers, thieves, and drug dealers. The more God revealed, the more my faith and awe in Him grew. I knew I was way out of my league and experience level. God guided my every step, my every move. I would have never believed anyone who told me that I might face such a battle in my life. I was in a world of characters that I had never before entertained or had experience with.

We must never underestimate the devastation of false assumptions or labeling. It is not accidental or some little innocent misstep. Human beings have lost their lives from the ugly deceit carried by assumptions. Even history has taught us this on several occasions, with devastating loss of life, and we still allow and even encourage this victimization of our fellow humans, and just go about our lives in the protected bubble provided for us. This is an unacceptable response, and it even carries responsibility for the so-called innocent bystanders who just turn their heads away from the problem. What creates such a willing appetite for false assumptions and labeling of others? What allows us to just so easily absorb false information accepted as truth? Beatrix first tapped into these skills at a very young age. Although she wasn't fully aware then, she developed the skill into what she needed to survive.

Beatrix on Transforming Assumptions into a Tool

I learned about assumptions from a very young age, and I had to live with their repercussions throughout my life. As fate has its way in our younger years, we are placed situationally beyond our control. We have no control over many things that are attributed to us, by which I mean our race, gender, religion, and/or socioeconomic status. This marks a clear distinction early on regarding our opportunities and the ease with which we live our lives. I am equally surprised each time I hear people so ignorantly say, "All people have the same opportunities." I pause and go into my head, attempting to decipher this statement, knowing that in a matter of seconds I could dismantle this thought. There is simply no truth to that statement. However, there is a sneaky little equalizer built into our universe that is there for the taking, but very few ever know how to access it. I was so excited when I made the discovery as to its access. I learned how to walk on any out-of-balance ground that I was forced to tread upon. I had to learn this concept at a young age and just kept honing it to get better at using it to correct injustice. I even learned to use it for advancement, when I wasn't marked to do so. I became an expert at this technique. I learned to exist unnoticed as a very young girl, blending into the group or in some cases becoming nearly invisible. Why would I have chosen such a tactic? Don't we all need and want validity in the world around us? I learned this technique accidentally and out of necessity. My family environment required this as a skill for survival. No, I wasn't saying to myself as a child, "You must be invisible." I learned its necessity, and then it became the normal state of existence. This is not the way in which one should acquire these skills; however, if you have lemons, make lemonade, right? It was imperative for me as a child to correctly read the landscape, understand its patterns, and then gauge how to proactively work with the conditions at hand. Quite simply, the more unnoticed I was, the better my day would be. But how does one exist in this type environment, and then learn to use the weaknesses against the system of oppression? It became a process of trial and error. I developed the ability to test the system, the unbalanced leadership, and then locate the opportunity to move within the system. Whenever you find yourself within this type of environment, you have but two paths of travel: succumb and accept the system, relying on the unbalanced leaders' favor of you; or, learn to work against the system, remaining under the radar, until you can exit the system of imbalance. My biggest decision regarding any ill-placed assumption became whether to act on it or just let it be. In most cases, doing nothing at all, swallowing my pride, was the correct action. I learned to take punches without flinching and then hold the negative energy of the opposition for later use. I experimented and tested many methods for cultivating the best resolve against the negativity of false assumptions created against me. At work, it took on the form of being passed over after delivering a consistently superior performance to that of the inferior coworker who just got slid into place with little to no effort at all. Many have experienced the same treatment regarding race, gender, socioeconomic biases, and so forth assigning them each to their box of rightful place.

I am equally frustrated when hearing people, the media, or leaders and politicians discussing the problems and prospective plans of attack. Plans that have been used numerous times, only to dig a bigger hole. It equates to a lot of noise, and keeps people confused and disillusioned. It's not that I haven't been guilty of misapplied efforts; I have. But, when that occurred, I used it as a lesson to propel me to a workable solution. I just can't, in all good conscience, watch in silence as people walk or are led to harm's way. Small problems have spread to become a malignant condition, and now they are rapidly revealing the diseased consequences.

We find ourselves up against problems compiled over time that haven't been effectively addressed. As we grow weary, tired, and frustrated, our responses worsen and revert to that which is comfortable. This outcome is to be expected if we have ignored problematic situations for a long time. We are living out such a disparity of thought, words, and actions. We have become completely out of balance, with an inner dysfunction of reasoning. This allows the outward imbalance to spin out of control. Could it be that we deliberately misrepresent facts? Or maybe we truly do not know the underlying truth at all. I think it is fair to say that it's a little bit of both. People react to the noise and emotional baggage, dragging them along and ensuring them a secured place in the future. There's no denying that the things people are fighting over held/hold true negatives toward others. However, our energy is best applied toward awareness, the root problems, and the fight needed. If you only address the *outcomes,* rather than the root, nothing will ever change and will surely worsen. Society is functioning in dangerous thought patterns and assumptions, rather than authentic information. This has always been the case at some level, since the beginning of time. But the more our world has enmeshed itself, melding our cultures, religions, economies and financial systems, it has become more pronounced and dangerous. We are wise in focusing on the part of the equation that is within the reach of change, rather than focusing on what we can no longer change because that window of time has already closed. We're better served directing our attention toward what can provide sustainable change. By creating more unity and collective buy-in, we will assume the responsibility and actions needed for necessary adjustments. In order to do this, we must be working on the authentic problems and the root from which the negatives stem. When there is no change, it points to a clue that you may be working on the wrong problem and/or using wrong approaches. This offers us a chance to go back to the drawing board and diligently seek out the root of a problem. This requires periods of questioning, examining, and testing the information being collected. Efforts will fail if you cannot properly collect, screen, and sift the information for relevance to the pending needs.

Exercise

What possible wrong assumptions have you experienced or witnessed? What was the result or outcomes attached to the false assumptions? Be specific and detailed in your responses so that you can see the level of danger and ugliness assumptions created.

Steps of Approach

Before launching the selected approach, be certain you have done the critical up-front work. This will assist you in drawing the best-possible conclusions. Be sure to leave room for error in your plan of approach. This will help guard your strategy against possible incorrect information as well as unknowns. So, be certain to build in room for error. For instance, while collecting data, it will become obvious if you are missing specifics. You may be forced to proceed anyway. Therefore, be just as aware of what you do not know as what you do know. By building safety nets around the unknowns, your mission will not be exposed or forced to abort. How, then, do we move into the next steps of approach? Approach becomes dictated by assumptions made regarding a situation, person, or thing. However, approach should be dictated by factual data rather than personality or beliefs. The moment you make it "about you," the approach becomes doomed to fail! So, if you find yourself thinking or saying things like "I think," stop right there, and redirect. You are about to sabotage your entire plan because of your own failed opinions and your ego. Remember, that approach is all about the other guy and not at all about you. You are just an instrument executing a methodical approach to yield a certain result or outcome. Carefully monitor your thoughts and speech as you are working out the approach. If you are making "I" statements, you will end up shaping an approach appealing to self rather than your subjects. It's not about you! I cannot emphasize this enough! Making it about you will lead you to unnecessary mistakes, wrong paths, and disaster for all. This critical mistake will lead to unwanted results. Other important elements to approach are what the truth tells you and what needs to be orchestrated at the "right" time. We tend to be in a hurry and react in knee-jerk fashions. It is imperative to learn how to discern our environments and the more important landscape of truth.

Noise versus Relevance

We are surrounded by external noise daily, and the ability to filter, ignore, and dump the irrelevant is a must. If not, you will struggle with having a controlled thought process that yields decisive and effective actions. To discern the relevant information from the irrelevant, you must first understand the difference between noise and that which is relevant. This is somewhat of an abstract concept and requires much practice. Let's talk about noise before we move on to the necessary steps of controlled thinking. By sorting and controlling the information you input, you drastically increase your chances and the effectiveness of your solutions. It's best to work through this process in a businesslike, methodical way, removing emotions and/or personal stances. This concept may not be fully understood by you; however, keep it in mind as you work through each of the steps. You will begin to see how both noise reduction and noise relevance naturally flow in the process of truthful discernment.

Let's Make a Deal

> "Or what king, when he sets out to meet another king in battle, will not first sit down and consider whether he is strong enough with ten thousand men to encounter the one coming against him with twenty thousand? "Or else, while the other is still far away, he sends a delegation and asks for terms of peace."
> —Luke 14:31–32 (NASB)

Negotiations are a critical and necessary part of all aspects of life. In young children, there is a natural built-in desire to get what they want, and they understand negotiations better than most adults. They turn on their sweet little smiles, perform cute little feats, all to distract you in order to change the outcome. Children are experts at manipulating every person and system to gain advantage and negotiate the deals they want. Slowly, as they grow, most of them will completely lose the ability to negotiate. Society will dampen and eventually remove this vital skill set in most of them. As described here, it seems like nothing more than manipulation, but that is basically what successful negotiations looks like. The difference lies in how and what it is used for, and that is what makes it good or bad. Parents use this technique every day, attempting to manipulate ideas of good behavior into their children and discourage bad behavior. This is an example of manipulation being used for good purpose. Keep in mind our earlier discussion of not becoming the tool you are using. Meaning that you should not strive to be a manipulative person, because that becomes destructive and highly deceptive. There is no alarm or worry needed if the tool selected is used for the actual good or protection of humankind. Earlier, we learned how Beatrix taught negotiation skills to her children from a very early age. She recognized the importance of allowing them to negotiate for what they wanted and encouraged their independent thinking. This is a tool of great importance for ourselves, our interactions in our communities, and the broader interactions of the world.

Recap of Beatrix's Negotiation Rules

1. You may disagree but do so respectfully and with meaningful evidence to support the idea.
2. Encourage others to plead their arguments, but this is only wise when they can support and back their arguments. Train your team to understand that the opposition will have a goal to break down their argument and outwit them *first!* Be, keenly aware, guarding all fences.

Beatrix

I knew it was of great importance for my children to learn all this early, while I could actively coach them on the how-tos and pitfalls of negotiations. I wanted it to become part of their own natural process. I explained to them that they should never enter a discussion or argument ill-informed, as this would destroy their ability to successfully negotiate a better outcome. Many parents discourage their children from disagreeing and certainly would not encourage them to negotiate. This is a critical skill set to instill in a child's life, one that will assist them throughout the entirety of their lives.

In my childhood home the rule was simple: "Do it because I said so."
There is certainly nothing wrong with having this rule; however,
it is critically flawed. The flaw occurs when you have a child like
me, who quietly understands when the parent is wrong in the
assessment or ruling. That child is dissecting everything around
him or her. When communication isn't an available option, that
child learns to create other ways to make things happen. Basically,
that child learns to negotiate deals. This can go in either a very
good or very bad direction, depending on the child. Successful
negotiations are profitable throughout our lives. So, as a parent, it
is wise to teach your children how to use negotiation for positive
reasons; otherwise, someone else may teach them to use it for
negative, undesirable, or even evil outcomes. A really bright child
will do this regardless of whether you choose to engage or not.
So, it is far better to "man the ship" as a parent. Children aren't
capable of doing this with their immature minds, but if you don't
do it, they will! We see this happening with our youth today. We
also see how ill-equipped they are, which is making more of them
turn to bad behaviors.

If you are not a good negotiator, this is a critical tool to acquire and
add to your tool belt. A basic rule for any successful negotiation
is understanding that it must be formed around what each party
needs or desires as an outcome. Whereas without negotiations,
worse conditions will exist for one party or both parties, it is wise
to be proactive in planning and framing the negotiation needed,
well in advance. The expert negotiator sees the future well in
advance and begins strategically positioning all parties toward
the desired outcome, without their awareness. They never feel a
thing; or, what they feel or perceive might be the "wrong" things.
Sound scary? It is! Especially when you have an "evil" negotiator
in your midst, or when you are unaware and ill prepared. That is
exactly why you must learn this powerful skill. To use this skill
with integrity, it must be coupled with honest and good motives.

It must never be used against people you love or any innocent person. Your foundational rules around this skill set should dictate its use, primarily in business or with an opposition that might have ill intentions toward others. As a strong reminder, you must never break your foundational rules, because when you do, you step into the trap of evil intentions. You then will set a trap for your own demise and destruction. It will also inhibit the ability to develop your skills as a master negotiator.

Beatrix, Master Negotiator

Throughout my years in business, I could maneuver in ways that "out negotiated" the evil intentions of those meaning harm. These were people who held much power, greater numbers, and more education than I did. It is up to you to establish your own foundational rules around this and all other skills, as truth dictates. After making your determinations and deciding on the course of action, how will you be able to negotiate the deal with others? Have you ever successfully negotiated a deal? How do you determine the wiggle room of where agreements can even be made? Then, how do you engage the characters into the positions for negotiations? In most cases, it's best that the characters never really understand that negotiations are under way. The better you become at applying these skills, the more likely that you will gain the advantage and remain unnoticed. This will be key for success in negotiating deals in such a way that the other party only has "one choice": the right choice you led them to conclude, but within their control. You see, we never can talk people into changing their minds; instead, we must carefully weave the answer into our approach, and, if done skillfully, they never attribute any idea to you. It has become an idea revealed to them, they buy in, and then you have succeeded in achieving the goal or change needed. This is a skillfully quiet tool, best used unnoticed, having the other party conclude that change is needed, welcomed, and ushered by them.

Now therefore, I beg you, swear to me by the Lord, since I have shown you kindness, that you also will show kindness to my father's house, and give me a true token, and spare my father, my mother, my brothers, my sisters, and all that they have, and deliver our lives from death." So the men answered her, "Our lives for yours, if none of you tell this business of ours. And it shall be, when the Lord has given us the land, that we will deal kindly and truly with you."

—Joshua 2:12–14 (NKJV)

I possess the mind of a criminal; if not for having a relationship with God, I am certain that I would not be a good person, perhaps even a very bad person. The scary thing about this is that I know God made others like me. And, if they do not serve a power bigger than that of self, inevitably, their gifts meant to assist man will be used for wicked deeds against humankind.

—Beatrix

All scripture is given by inspiration of God, and is profitable for doctrine, for reproof, for correction, for instruction in righteousness: That the man of God may be perfect, thoroughly furnished unto all good works.

—2 Timothy 3:16–17 (KJV)

Let brotherly love continue. Don't forget to show hospitality to strangers, for in doing so, some have entertained angels without knowing it.

—Hebrews 13:1–2 (WEB)

Chapter 7

Killer Released

Good Guys or Bad Guys?

So, who are the "bad guys"—the ones committing crimes against humankind and upsetting the world? We are inundated daily by news shows, along with the opinions of our families and communities, as to which people are the bad guys and which are the good guys. The trouble with this method is that all we have is finger-pointing, followed by hate-filled actions or attitudes. We aren't succeeding at developing actionable plans to remedy anything. It isn't that we have new problems, but, rather, just a festering of old problems that, unattended, grew and morphed into a monster. Meaning, the old problems keep transforming their shape and appearance, so what we avoid or ignore never goes away. There is no such thing as sweeping problems under the rug. They only grow and morph into something completely new. Even then, we don't see the ugly monster in our midst and about to destroy us. So, it continues to grow stronger and bigger, and eventually it becomes unmanageable. Humankind has slowly grown to accept propaganda as truth. This will lead to the fall of humanity, and it was avoidable. People aren't born bad. Rather, they are born into bad circumstances, with little or no tools to assist them. It is rare that people will choose to make choices seemingly paradoxical to the community in which they reside. This can create conflict with those in their social environment, so it becomes easier to keep their heads down and follow the crowd. And then, there are those, regardless of socioeconomic state, who truly do not have the capability of seeing the full reality. They are actually and innocently ignorant, because they did not choose it. It's part of the cards they hold. However, most people *choose* ignorance, pretending to be dumb in regard to the matters at hand. The matter of intelligence does not lie within socioeconomic sectors; perhaps education does, but not intelligence. So, the people who truly are ignorant of certain factors hold no guilt. This is not true or a luxury for the men or women who can be aware. From a moral and ethical standard, this places us all on a level playing field in the realm of spirituality. God built in balance and fairness for the body of humanity. It is humankind that has destroyed the balance! We cannot fool God; He always knows our authentic makeup and motives. If we were given more, then more responsibility and action will be required from us. This is not just by way of money, but also talents and abilities of all kinds. We were sent to serve His purpose, and we will be judged individually based on what He knew we had the ability to do while here. From a biblical study point, read Luke, chapter 12, in its entirety; it explains this concept in full. Here are two of my favorite verses from this chapter:

> The servant who knows the master's will and does not get ready or does not do what the master wants will be beaten with many blows. But the one who does not know and does things deserving punishment will be beaten with few blows. From everyone who has been given much, much will be demanded; and from the one who has been entrusted with much, much more will be asked. (Luke 12:47–48 NIV)

Hopefully, you took time to read all of Luke, chapter 12. If so, you will gain a broader conceptual view of this discussion. The viewpoints we have adopted from one another, and our role in the overall care of one another, have been transformed into the deadly ideas and actions we see playing out in society. This is a result of our faulty thinking; that applies even to those who claim to know God. It is particularly harmful from that group, and so it holds more accountability with God in terms of judgment. Believers should be striving to grow and live out the principles required of them. Instead, they have chosen to follow the standards and actions of society, relieving themselves of responsibility. This also results in a blocked ability to access the power and wisdom that God meant for them.

Society tells us to stay with our own kind and on our own little piece of real estate. Anyone outside of our bubble of design becomes marked as the "ones to keep our eye on." We begin to see "them" as crossing the lines and bending the standards of the rules we set. We mark those who act more in accordance with the teachings of Jesus as bad, even traitors. We begin an attempt at setting the crowd on a full-blown attack against them. We easily follow the pack mentality. We somehow value the judgment or mere men and women around us as superior to that of God. Is this different from those who spit on Jesus, abused and mocked Him? This eventually led to His death, ultimately caused by the very people He loved and served. He could have changed it, but He didn't, because of love. He knew they did not fully understand what they were doing. We choose to place or leave our fellow humans in certain circumstances, claiming that these cannot be changed. We still claim God as our Lord and Savior. Can you see the conflict here? Can you see how misshaped the minds and actions of humankind have become? Does this mean we believe ourselves to be superior to God? Do we feel that we have a right to impart our judgment and rules to serve our own purposes rather than His? Are our own judgments better than those of God?

Although we may think this occurs more in the lower socioeconomic levels, it occurs just as much among the rich and the middle class. It takes on different shapes and forms, but all are still equal in effect. We have allowed society to shape our minds around the idea of "good people," who really aren't that good at all; they are just packaged as society says good should look. And then, the "bad" aren't always as bad as we might think they are. Society has set rules and standards around what is considered normal. In most cases, this causes much more harm to humankind than the pettier bad seen among those in lower socioeconomic classes. Society brainwashes our minds into the us-against-them mentality. And we swallow it hook, line, and sinker! We seem to feel unsatisfied without an enemy, so we create one—or, we allow our leaders to determine and define them for us. This has resulted in much fighting among ourselves.

What can we learn about the true life of how Jesus walked while on the earth? He didn't come from royal blood, and only one of the twelves disciples was believed to be of royal blood. Jesus was a common man, and He chose common men—even men with criminal histories—to be His chosen disciples. Why would He have acted in such a paradoxical way? Why did He choose people whom most of the prestigious so-called believers wouldn't be caught dead among? Gentle Jesus, meek and mild. It's a distortion, but a pervasive one. Such is the power of song and poetry. People want to believe that. It's dangerous. Moreover, it simply isn't true. Jesus was a tenderhearted man. There were times when He chose to be meek. But He was never mild. He was born into conflict and remained in it His whole life. He jousted with the devil in the desert; He frequently exchanged words with the religious groups of the day. He risked life and reputation by spending time with housefuls of tax collectors and in the company of known prostitutes. He was not condemned to die on the cross because He was mild.

Wild is a better description, meaning He did things that seemed unusual and paradoxical for results. Onlookers were undoubtedly surprised and frustrated by His unusual approaches. This does not mean wild in the fashion used to describe an unruly lifestyle. He was wild enough to turn over the tables of those who were fleecing the faithful as they came to the temple to worship. He was wild enough to embrace the hated neighbors (Samaritans). He was wild enough to touch the unclean leper.

Jesus was meek and *wild*. Are you comfortable with that paradox? It is a challenge to our normal, either/or mind-set. Is it possible to believe that Jesus's life was full of both paradoxes and tensions? What does scripture tell us?

He worked with His father as a carpenter. He fell asleep in boats during storms. He ate, He wept, He cried out in anguish as the time of His trial approached. He was moved with compassion for His friends Lazarus, Mary, and Martha.

Jesus was very human.

But Jesus was divine. His earthly mother Mary was impregnated by the Divine. Jesus was the Son of God. He talked to His Father constantly.

The record of His life speaks of His authority over the elements of nature. He walked on the water. He rebuked the wind and the raging waters, and they became calm.

He rose from the dead, was seen by more than five hundred witnesses and extended His nail-pierced hands to the doubting disciple Thomas.

How do we reconcile His divinity and His humanity? How could they coexist? If we allow for the reality of the human/divine in the person of Jesus, what other tensions might we allow?

Jesus seemed to care little for popular opinion. He warned healed people not to gossip about what had happened to them. He risked the wrath of the whole city of Jericho by visiting the tax collector whom everyone hated, even musing that some of the crowds following Him were spiritual thrill-seekers from a "wicked generation."

This prophetic confrontation was a hallmark of Jesus's words and deeds.

But what kind of toughness did it take to hear people attribute His miracles to the devil, to walk through crowds ready to throw you over a cliff, or to endure the lashes that should never have been given to an innocent man?

What kind of man would die the slow death of suffocation to which hanging from the cross sentenced you?

What kind of man would return to a group of men who had betrayed Him and make the most verbal traitor the leader of His new community? What kind of man would step nimbly around the verbal traps laid by His opponents, seeking to get Him to disagree with the law of Moses or the tax laws of the day?

Not a weak man, not a timid man, not a man who lacked principles, and not a man whose life was held captive by the opinions of others.

Jesus was tough because He was compassionate. One led to the other. He had come to take captivity captive. He had come to release the oppressed.

Are you ready to confront systems of thought with the challenge of the life and words of Jesus? Are you willing to express an unpopular opinion and face the anger and misrepresentation of your motives that will result? Can you live with the tension of seeking to balance that mental toughness with a gracious kindness to people seeking to make sense of their lives and circumstances? It is vital that we do. Impatience and a judgmental attitude are the curse of the prophet who doesn't internalize the wisdom of the whole of Jesus's life. Are you willing to embrace the paradox of grace and justice?

Have we grown so blind as to truly believe that our political party of choice, some politician, or enforcement of laws old and new will turn the tide and change our disastrous chosen path? Can any one of us claim to hold the solution, or is the solution divine in nature, when it comes to changing the hearts and minds of humankind? Some will hear, and others will continue to deny Him; nevertheless, all will bow to Him—either now, while we can still serve, or later, upon judgment of our failures. May each man and woman seek their hearts with great intent.

Jesus between the Criminals

Crucifixion in the ancient world was intended to take as long as possible. No vital organs were damaged, so it took two or three days to die, often from shock or asphyxiation, as muscles used for breathing grew weak.

Luke 23:39–43 is a conversation between Jesus and the criminals crucified alongside him, and it is in the Bible because crucifixion was slow. There was time to talk. This conversation is surely one of the most extraordinary in the Bible. It shows us the similarities of these three dying men; and yet, at the same time, how very different Jesus is.

The First Criminal

The first criminal speaks to Jesus with bitter sarcasm: "Are you not the Christ? Save yourself and us!"

His words betray a terrible misunderstanding. He says to Jesus, "Save yourself and us!" The criminal is talking about salvation from the physical agony of crucifixion. But he doesn't understand that it's precisely by staying on the cross and not saving Himself that Jesus is able to save others from God's judgment, a fate far worse than physical death. Saving Himself is the one thing Jesus must not do. Instead, He must surrender Himself. He must bear God's wrath if we are to avoid it. His death doesn't call into question His claim to be the Messiah. It proves it.

The Second Criminal

The second criminal rebukes the first. He points out how all three men are the same: "Do you not fear God, since you are under the same sentence of condemnation?" They have all been condemned to death by Rome. But there is also a crucial difference. The two criminals deserve to die, while Jesus doesn't: "this man has done nothing wrong." Even though Jesus is suffering the same Roman judgment and the same physical pain as the criminals, He is the sinless one who doesn't deserve it.

But Jesus is different in another way, too—one that the second criminal misses. Jesus's sentence of condemnation goes way beyond Roman punishment. On the cross, Jesus is condemned by God Himself. He is "smitten by God," and "the Lord has laid on him the iniquity of us all." The two criminals bear Rome's judgment. Jesus bears Rome's judgment *and* God's judgment. Though His sin is infinitely less, His punishment is infinitely greater.

Jesus

Finally, Jesus speaks. The second criminal had said, "Jesus, remember me when you come into your kingdom." Jesus replies, "Truly, I say to you, today you will be with me in Paradise." Jesus decides who goes to heaven. And it turns out to be very good news for this criminal that Jesus is so different from him. Because Jesus is innocent and bears God's judgment (not just Rome's judgment), He can make a way for the criminal to be with him—forever. Their difference is the criminal's salvation. Jesus dies so the criminal can live. He bears hell on the cross so the criminal doesn't need to bear it forever.

The Results

What's the result of this conversation between the three crucified men?

The first criminal bears Roman condemnation on the cross and then God's condemnation forever. And he deserves both.

The second criminal bears Roman condemnation on the cross but no condemnation from God forever. He deserves the first, while the second is a free gift.

Jesus, though He deserves neither Rome's condemnation nor God's condemnation, bears both on the cross. And so, He secures for the second criminal—who is every bit as bad as the first—the free gift of eternal life.

Both the topic and teachings regarding the paradoxical ways of Jesus serve to offer us new insights into what we misunderstood, or thought we understood. Many believers find this subject to be taboo, perhaps even evil. But, when you study it more carefully, it yields such a comforting truth that many believers miss. By the misunderstanding among believers, we create a great divide for those who might come. We become a stumbling block to those around us, and we may even work counter to God's will, inadvertently more in favor of the will of dark powers. Those very teachings that seem paradoxical represent the freedom, fairness, love, mercy, and forgiveness for all, removing any right we thought we had in judging others.

A Dark Stranger Appears

Beatrix

Who is this man, and where did he come from? And why is he in my world? Oh my goodness, he is terrifying. I could sense the dark energy envelop me in his presence. *Why is this man in my path? Where did he suddenly come from?* I asked myself these questions for some time, all the while trying to shoo him away. After all, this is one of my strengths, shooing people away. But he wouldn't go. He was unaffected by all of my attempts. I kept thinking, *What? Seriously?!* But, he kept appearing, chuckling and telling me corny jokes. I had to laugh, of course. He was a mystery, and I do love "the solve." But there was more, something underlying, and I knew I needed to answer that question. Something wasn't right here!

I was taken aback at how he just laughed off my polite attempts to have him go. Very curious, which was unusual, because I find most to be quite predictable. *Hmm, I will just ignore him, and he'll get tired.* Except he didn't. I became drawn to this strange character, and to the meaning of it all. Was I completely outside of my realm? Our characters were like night and day; yet I saw something else in him, and that's the thing that drew me in for a closer look. Rarely challenged by people, the thought of one who was challenging me became magnetic in force. *No way, he is scary!* Of course, I told him that he scared me. It only amused him.

So, I began to pray, as I always did when someone appeared in my path who really shouldn't be there at all. I keep praying about this crazy guy. And what did I finally hear? Well, I really doubted it. It couldn't be right. It was just too bizarre! However, the same answer kept coming back. I keep hearing, "Beatrix, get along beside of him. He will protect you." Protect me from what? I felt totally disturbed by this, so I waited and did nothing. In my mind, this could only spell trouble for me; except I did not yet know the trouble that lay ahead for me and my family. If you would have told me then how this man would protect and shield me from so many things that came, I would have never believed it. How could this man hold such conflicting natures within him? What had seemed like just some scary guy would turn out to be both a blessing and curse for us both. Our friendship grew; we both seemed to understand one another—or at least that we needed to understand more. I am sure we both questioned the same things. He was very guarded, and so was I. But he was hurting, he was hurting so badly; I never let on that I noticed, because I understood him. I knew it would hurt him if he knew I saw his pain. He needed the tough exterior for protection. I didn't dare let on that I noticed. I continued to pray for understanding, and God kept nudging me to just "get beside of him." Just in presence. I had no idea why, but it was consistent and firm: "Get beside of him!" Ultimately, I did just that.

Was he a good guy or a bad guy? He was a good guy to me; he was the best guy! This dark stranger helped me conquer what I could not do alone, and I in turn helped him conquer what he needed to conquer. Did God know that I would be able to see him, the real guy hidden inside? The healing that was possible, through a series of unfolding events? Did God know that this guy would see me, even though no one else ever had? And did God know that this unlikely crossing of paths would allow "others to be seen" and then "others to finally see?" Can our minds ever attempt to imagine what one act of obedience or kindness can alter in infinite ways, rippling across the water, impacting the lives of many, even ones' unknown to us? And, if not obedient, even when scared, facing danger, unsure, confused, can we begin to imagine the negative impacts in the lives of others because we chose disobedience?

The power of this story, and the dark stranger Beatrix never should have met, illustrates a very provoking thought. The paths of these two people were unlikely to ever cross, but somehow, they did anyway. I can assure you that Beatrix was legitimately afraid of what the dark stranger represented to her. By her own accord, she would have never gotten closer to him or the situations that followed without instruction or heeding obediently to the repeated instruction of the God she served. She knew that she was in unfamiliar and dangerous territory. She couldn't fathom such an outrageous request from God. Their story became one of conquering dangers that most only believe to be in the movies. You know, the movie content that puts you on the edge of your seat. A don't-blink-an-eye type of movie! Beatrix grew to understand exactly why God had requested this dangerous and lonely journey of her. Through that understanding not only was she grateful for the journey, she was also fearful of the many thoughts she had of denying the request of God. She imagined what the horrific consequences of that failure might have held for many.

This is one of the most important reasons why Beatrix wanted to tell her story. She grew to understand the critical importance of walking in complete faith and obedience. She knew that her disobedience would have resulted in harm to others and dire consequences for her. These two strangers, opposite both in nature and social affiliations, would unlock the killer inside of Beatrix, and the good inside the dark stranger. The impact extended to the enemies they faced and to many innocent victims. Beatrix tapped the killer instincts within. We all want to find the strength within that can allow us to overcome and conquer challenges for ourselves and others. Beatrix explained how she now understood, without doubt, that God wanted to place her close enough to a certain set of circumstances. In doing so, she would have the opportunity to discover things needing her skills. She could have refused, and He would have found another. But her refusal would not have gone without consequence. Her choice of obedience did lead to certain consequences; however, she knew with certainty that if she would have refused, many would have suffered a far greater harm. And, her own consequences would have been much worse. There was a buried, much-deeper problem, having little to do with her. Circumstances and characters that seemed unrelated were brought together for purpose. She grew to understand that their paths had been divinely crossed. An entanglement of her son opened doorways that Beatrix would have never walked through. Did God know exactly how Beatrix would respond to these circumstances involving her child? Did He allow the entanglement, leading her to a much bigger set of problems otherwise unknown to her? These problems became a very dangerous and life-threatening situation for Beatrix. She came to understand that neither her son nor she would have survived if not for the dark stranger.

I will attempt to find words to properly explain the passion Beatrix feels about having others understand the way in which God revealed himself to her. A completely new way, an intimate way. A way in which anyone seeking could also obtain. He was no longer an obscure object that she read about and served; He was her most intimate friend. He guided her safely through a five-year period of fiery furnaces. She got bruised and banged up but was able to access the power only God can offer. Take heed these words I am saying carefully: God brought her through danger most of us will never experience in a lifetime. She experienced numerous attempts on her life, and God blocked all the attempts. He allowed her to use the skills and abilities He had given her and groomed within in the years prior. Some believed she had made a deal with the devil and left her God. Instead, Beatrix had made the deal with God before beginning her journey. She understood that her life might have been required in the saving of her son. She accepted that outcome as the lesser in consequence. Each day reminded her of the likelihood of that reality.

Even bystanders and those meaning harm to Beatrix witnessed firsthand the miraculous power of God. They had the power and the numbers on their side. Beatrix was a simple woman with no one to shield her. God became her shield, and He sent her teammates to help her through this dangerous and difficult time. Another reveal happened through this time: the reveal of Beatrix, because of the battle she had to face and fight alone; it allowed Beatrix to be seen for who she really was. Beatrix understood that this spelled even more danger for her. In order to conquer, she was forced to lay all her cards on the table, revealing her authentic self. Beatrix had no desire to reveal just how otherworldly smart she was in the skills and talents she became forced to use. The more aware people became of her abilities, the greater the danger grew, and there was no way to put the worms back into the can. God had revealed her for all to see, and this only spelled more trouble for Beatrix. This spelled greater danger for her, because people now began to blame Beatrix for events she had nothing to do with. Once they saw how smart she was in these specific skills and talents, she became a marked woman to take out. Beatrix always had understanding that true power should not, and typically will not, reveal itself. The guilty parties witnessed the power of God at work, but, wishing to deny it, they chose a more digestible thought, and blamed Beatrix. They didn't want to see the mighty power, if this God thing was true. That would spell new ideas, challenges, and changes in store for them. Hurting Beatrix was a more comfortable alternative for them. This alternative required nothing different from them. It allowed them to remain in their standard mode of operating. Beatrix became the easier target for them, and they could dismiss the God thing entirely. Beatrix knew the power wasn't hers; she kept explaining this to any who would hear. She understood she wasn't capable of any great feats without God's exact timing and instructions and walking submissively in obedience and faith. She understood the great danger that surrounded her, and daily reaffirmed the deal she made with God. Her awareness of the deal she made kept her in prayer and quiet meditation daily, seeking His quiet voice, and pleading with Him for guidance, strength, endurance, ability, and a hedge of protection for the tasks.

Did God give Beatrix more than she could handle? For her, it felt as if He had; however, He knew things about Beatrix that she did not. What kept Beatrix going, even after she experienced those making attempts on her life? How was she able to look the devil and death in the eye, and say, "Shoot!" It was the deal she made with God for the love of her son. It soon became a host of other discoveries! There was no turning back. Her fear of the consequences of quitting was far greater than danger or death. At the very least, she knew she would go to a better place. But, if she chose disobedience, she would be alive to watch others suffer when she could have helped. She would face the great consequences of not obeying the voice of God spoken to her for the greater good of others. She knew that nothing faced through this walk would be as bad as that. She told me how she would visualize facing God, and what He might say to her if she denied him. This was not something to risk, so anything else she might face would be far less costly. She knew if she broke her deal, her son would be lost, and nowhere in her heart could her own life be above the safety of her son or family. In her usual method of "this" or "that" thinking, she knew that her deal with God meant that she had to do "this", all of "this," without questions, no matter the consequences. But the price she could not afford was "that"—the price of losing her son. The "that" of refusing God's instruction and being accountable for the harm done to others. It was a cost she simply could not afford. She had done all the before steps before setting out on her approach and journey. She came to realize that all her earlier years of struggle and refining of skills helped her succeed and survive. Were all the earlier and difficult times a time of preparing for this war? Had God carefully intertwined the lives of many for His divine purpose? Had He set the stage with the characters needed? Had he brought together others also possessing well-refined talents and abilities from early years of struggle and endurance? I can tell you this was, and still is, the true belief of Beatrix. If Beatrix would have depended on what she understood, would she still be alive today? Would her entire family have suffered great harm if she had disobeyed? God gave Beatrix a vision and His instruction—not just once, but over and over, until she finally moved in obedience. As she described it, "He told me my family would not survive, and that they would be needed in the future." Beatrix didn't go around telling this to anyone; she knew no one would ever believe her. She said that God commanded her silence. She didn't fully understand what God wanted from her, but she knew that obedience was required. The more she obeyed, the more God revealed to Beatrix. The more He revealed, the more frightening the reality became, because He proved *all* in *truth* that she previously doubted.

The *authentic* Beatrix was positioned on the front line of a war. It released her killer instincts. A proverbial killer set loose for God's purpose, a purpose having little to do with Beatrix. She became a mere tool for God to access, for a specific calling, and a specific time. God knew this day would be in the path of Beatrix, and He had been preparing her all along the way, even when she was discouraged and hopeless. He knew! Beatrix, even after facing all of this, felt so grateful for this war; for through it, she discovered the real God, and an intimate connection to Him. She discovered He is nothing like what our humanness paints Him to be. Her most sincere desire is that others will understand that there is more, much more, for their access. The keys that unlocked this new level of being with Christ, a true intimacy with the Father, came in the form of war and danger. It was revealed by loving another/others more than herself, and deciding to walk in swift obedience, complete faith, and even unto death if required. And the dark stranger, the seeming "bad guy," was sent by God alone to fight alongside of Beatrix, in a war bigger than either of them could have imagined. Two strangers who would have never met unless a Higher Power had caused their paths to cross.

Beatrix on the Tutelage of a "Bad Guy"

I guess I've never been too afraid of anything. You learn to live with fear when it's all you've ever known. Even when I felt fear, I would quietly say to myself, "Yeah, you think you got something for me?" (Chuckle.) "You don't know who raised me!"

I had already survived far worse than most could ever do to me. Funny thing, though: the very things that should have broken me, and almost did a few times, became tools that I learned to use to power through any obstacle I faced. I would remind myself of what God had already brought me through, pull up my bootstraps, keep pushing, and keep fighting!

My father always loved to brag about how he had us "broke," as he put it. You may hear that and think that maybe we were unruly kids. We weren't. We were fearful kids, nervous kids, kids who learned to walk on eggshells daily. We walked the line. The fear was so great that we never dared to do anything to set off any explosion. My sister Anna and I talked privately about what we needed to do to keep things calmer for our mother—and to ensure our survival. As a child, my father looked like a monster to me. He loved to proclaim that he was mean. He bragged about it. I guess that was meant as a reinforcement so that we would never think of crossing him. He was certainly a man of his word; he wasn't bluffing. He had backed it up enough times that we understood there were no limits to his tactics. We lived in a hidden nightmare every day.

He loved to brag about his wild and rowdy days to anyone who would listen to him. It was like a badge of honor to him. He said he had never apologized to anyone and was doggone proud of it! It was so hard to live such double lives. No one ever knew what was going on behind closed doors. We would go out in public, watching the hero worship people gave him, watching him doting on other children. It made me sick watching him being sickeningly sweet, kissing their checks, and even giving them each a dollar to put in their pockets. It was all part of "the show." And then, observing the parents of these kids, seeing the twinkle in their eyes for this man, our daily tormentor. But, as strange as this may sound, I still loved him. I wanted his attention. I wanted him to give me, my mother, and my siblings the love he was giving these strangers, but that would never happen. Still, I always remained hopeful.

One of many troubling episodes for Anna and me occurred one evening after going to bed. We were awoken to the sounds of our mother pleading with our father, and yet another verbal battering of our mother and Kay, our older sister. We lay there, nervous and afraid, chewing our nails to the quick, not knowing what we should do. We were terrified of our father. But we decided to crawl quietly down the hallway to see if Kay and our mom were okay. We crawled slowly and quietly down the hall, and then under the kitchen table, so that we could get close enough to hear but not be seen. Time stood still. I can't even say how long we were under that table, but then he heard us. Now we were all there in front of this madman. I can't even really explain to you what this is like for a child. You are so afraid, but it somehow becomes normal, and it remains hidden from the outside world. You protect your abuser, the very one who is threatening you. It breaks you down little by little, until you are under that person's complete control. The only goal is to survive.

Well, there we were, just sitting in front of him, terrified, while he ranted at us. He promised that the next morning, he would shoot us in the back while we went to get on the bus, and then he would shoot himself. We left that night—as I'll explain in a moment—and if we hadn't left that night, we would have slowly walked to that bus and let him do it. We would have let him shoot us. Not one of us would have dared question him. That is the degree of control and fear he held us hostage.

By the grace of God, he fell asleep, and we left for a few days, running from house to house, our mother putting us in closets to hide us when she thought he was coming. The escape was short-lived. We returned to an even more volatile boiling pot; my mom had crossed a line with him by taking us from him. This became a weapon he used to create more guilt and more fear, ensuring that we would walk the line. The foregoing scenario was just one of many violent occurrences where our lives were on the line.

I wish I could explain how we came to have to give him the same worship he required from everyone else in his presence. We all wanted to be in his favor, because if you weren't, the consequences were great. That even created divisions among all of us: me, my sisters, and my mom. Even that was by design; the infighting was his way of keeping himself, the abuser, in control. Basically, it was a matter of divide and conquer. The distrust that grew among us was just another layer of destruction he designed against us.

Even scarier than that was when he was taking us all to the mountains, planning to run the car off the side of the mountain to our deaths. As an adult, when I think now about our solution to that, I am both confused and shocked, but that is what these environments do to people. You begin to operate on a completely different level in your mind. There is one thought, one goal: *survive one more day.* The solution my mother came up with is a perfect example of this. She was so desperate, she called her mother (my grandmother) to go with us. Now, I don't know what my mother explained to my grandmother, if anything at all. But having her mother come along was the only solution that my mother could come up with. This man didn't care about his own life, and he certainly wouldn't have allowed us to remain alive free from his control. My mother knew he was just crazy enough to do it. I can't even explain to you the level of fear I felt that day, even greater than ever before, perhaps because I was older and could comprehend more.

So, as we wound around curvy mountain roads, my father kept singing these sick, twisted songs of how he was going to run us over the mountain. He just continued singing, louder and louder, to increase our terror. My grandmother kept trying to distract him by keeping him talking. She probably did save us that day. That was just a tiny wrench that upset the plan that had been carefully mapped out in his head. We survived again, at least physically. The scars he was leaving inside all of us were traumatic and deep.

Through all of this, I still so wanted him to love me, to be my friend, but that never happened. Instead, he had great animosity toward me, mostly because he could tell that I wasn't mentally broken to him as he wanted. I certainly never told him this or talked back to him in any way, but he knew. Guys who operate like this always know how to brainwash and control those around them. It's no accident. And they can always tell if someone is not completely on board with them. That person becomes their target. They can usually only have one favorite, whom they carefully select. In our family, that was Anna. My older sister, Kay, and I became his in-house targets. These guys always have targets. Their sick minds constantly plan out punishment for what they consider to be transgressions, which I can tell you not one us ever committed. We were dutifully obedient and even protective of him. But there is no logic in these types of environments.

Was my father a bad guy? In the sense of his actions and behaviors, he was. But I also knew he was full of pain and suffering. He, too, had been hurt deeply. It became very conflicted in my mind, because he acted like a completely different guy while at church and behind the pulpit. I would keep trying to explain it away in my mind, making excuses for why he treated us so badly. And our mother certainly told us all the reasons why he behaved in these ways, and then we started feeling sorry for him again. We would feel guilty for our feelings. The version of altered reality became our "truth." This furthered the thought that we did not matter. Our confusion was transformed into there being "something wrong with us"! Our feelings did not matter. My siblings and I lived for our parents' feelings, for their life. Everything revolved around our father, the protection of our mother, and the church, which I grew to hate. My siblings and I beat ourselves up, because all children love their parents and so desperately want their love in return. There is no possible way for children to reason in this environment. It all comes back on them as blame.

As an adult, I can see that my father was a man full of pain and suffering, who somehow was never able to access the tools he needed for healing. I can say a million reasons why, but no one truly has the answer except him. Yet, even now, I hold on to hope for his healing and for my sisters' healing. The healing never came for my mother; she died in that sad state.

I never lost hope that perhaps, one day, we could at least have authentic relationships, rather than needing to tiptoe around land mines. Even now, when I visit him, I never know what to expect. Will this visit be okay, or will he attack me or my children? Or, will I walk into a baited trap, where he plays nice because he knows you want that, and when you bite, he changes into the devil once again? It's very much like Jekyll and Hyde. I cannot express how much this grieves my heart, maybe because I still desire a better relationship with him. Or, maybe I just want to see him more at peace. It's difficult looking back at how our lives were overcome with dysfunction and pain. I love him, but I can no longer expose myself to his mistreatment. The unfortunate truth is, our parents stole our lives from us, even in adulthood. I still long for healing and peace for all of us.

> "So you will find favor and good repute In the sight of God and man. Trust in the LORD with all your heart, And do not lean on your own understanding. In all your ways acknowledge Him, And He will make your paths straight."
>
> —Proverbs 3:4–6 (NASB)

Bad Guys against Change

When you begin the process of change, expect a fight until the finish line. You will be fighting the old you, along with a host of characters sent to stop your movement. You must calculate for this before ever setting out on a planned approach. They will come! Who are these characters that I speak of? They are best identified as the "wagon circlers." Their job is to *stop you,* and if you are lackadaisical toward or unaware of this factor, expect to fail. They are coming for you! I wrote a blog about this awhile back, putting it in a funny, but proper, perspective.

Beware of "Wagon Circlers"

They're comin', I tell ya! They're a-comin'! The very moment of the tiniest step toward change, and you will find yourself in the dusty cloud of smoke, hearing their triggers clicking ... aimed right at our heads! This *always happens,* so we must be aware. We must be ready to respond to their reactions, well planned and prepared. Wagon circlers have made careers and amassed great wealth, just because they understand the power and emotional response of this mind game Most people don't even know what is happening, much less see them a-comin'. Some basic rules to guide us in dealing with wagon circlers:

1. Change is *always* an unwelcome visitor.
2. Change makers take great risks, oftentimes involving personal danger.
3. Wagon circlers have but one goal: stop the Change! They will stop at nothing. They will go to the lowest below-the-belt positions to initiate their attacks. All for their own selfish reasons and insecurities. We must recognize their approach and be in position, ready and prepared to fight.

This battle has been going on for years. The legend goes something like this: The dusty old Cowboy of Change comes riding into town on his weathered, worn, ol' saddle. (He's been in a few wagon-circling battles.) He's a seasoned sharpshooter with the mind of a ninja warrior. He (or, perhaps, she) is an odd character of sorts, and that is where it begins. The wagon circlers begin to circle, offering a personal attack against Cowboy Change and his unusual ways. They build fear and skepticism in the onlookers. They convince the onlookers of some devious plot or threat that the cowboy has in store for them. They look back at the cowboy, and fear strikes their hearts and minds. They begin to talk among themselves, pointing their fingers at the oddities evidenced against Cowboy Change. He is one mysterious and strange hombre. Before long, new and different stories are created, quickly growing out of control and spreading like a wildfire. Meanwhile, the wagon circlers chuckle to themselves, admiring their handiwork. Once again, they have stopped the possibility of change before the ol' cowboy can jump off his horse. No one likes change! People say they want it, but they do not have the heart or willingness to see it to fruition. Once people can see and acknowledge the truth as it really is, it requires things of them. New choices will have to be made at the expense of things given up in order to produce the change. Their fears set in. They wanted the change, but they didn't agree to participate or give anything up now. So, they look back over at the wagon circlers. Then they look back at Cowboy Change, with doubt in their hearts and minds. They look again at the wagon circlers. The wagon circlers give them little winks and nods, convincing them, once again, that "they have what they need," and no sacrifice at all will be required. The onlookers look around at one another suspiciously. They declare, "Yeah, who does that Cowboy Change think he is?" They keep discussing it among themselves, each one feeding the other with support of the idea of getting something for nothing That sounds pretty good!

Before long, they run Cowboy Change slap out of town. But this won't stop Cowboy Change. He just climbs back into his dusty ol' saddle, moving on to the next town, hoping that the next time … just maybe … the people will be able to discern, decide, and embrace the very change they have been praying for. You see, Cowboy Change can't stop. It's his very essence of being. He has no shiny objects to offer. He didn't come to steal, cheat, or lie to the people, unlike the wagon circlers, but he realizes just how hard it is for people to accept and work for change. Cowboy Change knows the time is coming when people will run themselves out of options. Cowboy Change just hopes they wake up before it's too late. He rides on in peace, doing no harm, knowing the day for change is somewhere else on his dusty trail. He rides off into the sunset just as mysteriously as he rode into town, remembering the people all along his journey. Maybe one day, just maybe … the pain of destruction of the wagon circlers will reveal itself as the worse enemy, the more dangerous threat to people. Convincing the onlookers/people that its deception and destruction is far greater than anything given up for change, survival, and thriving. He prepares for the day when the wagon circlers will have broken one too many promises, told one too many lies, and thieved the people on too many occasions, making them slaves for mere bread and water. Cowboy Change only has the rugged raw truth, but he loves the people. He loves the people enough to stand with them when the time comes. The time for change! Ride on, Cowboy.

Praise to the God of All Comfort

Paul, an apostle of Christ Jesus by the will of God, and Timothy our brother, To the church of God in Corinth, together with all his holy people throughout Achaia: Grace and peace to you from God our Father and the Lord Jesus Christ. Praise be to the God and Father of our Lord Jesus Christ, the Father of compassion and the God of all comfort, who comforts us in all our troubles, so that we can comfort those in any trouble with the comfort we ourselves receive from God. For just as we share abundantly in the sufferings of Christ, so also our comfort abounds through Christ. If we are distressed, it is for your comfort and salvation; if we are comforted, it is for your comfort, which produces in you patient endurance of the same sufferings we suffer. And our hope for you is firm, because we know that just as you share in our sufferings, so also you share in our comfort. We do not want you to be uninformed, brothers and sisters, about the troubles we experienced in the province of Asia. We were under great pressure, far beyond our ability to endure, so that we despaired of life itself. Indeed, we felt we had received the sentence of death. But this happened that we might not rely on ourselves but on God, who raises the dead. He has delivered us from such a deadly peril, and he will deliver us again. On him we have set our hope that he will continue to deliver us, as you help us by your prayers. Then many will give thanks on our behalf for the gracious favor granted us in answer to the prayers of many. Now this is our boast: Our conscience testifies that we have conducted ourselves in the world, and especially in our relations with you, with integrity and godly sincerity. We have done so, relying not on worldly wisdom but on God's grace. For we do not write you anything you cannot read or understand. And I hope that, as you have understood us in part, you will come to understand fully that you can boast of us just as we will boast of you in the day of the Lord Jesus.

—2 Corinthians 1:1–14 (NIV)

Become the Label Assigned to You

To be the label assigned to you seems to run counter to the message of ripping off the labels assigned to you. By now, you have discovered the paradoxical nature of Beatrix that allowed her to think, approach, and solve problems that many others pass over as impossible. Her rare and misunderstood approach to things became the exact formula needed to infiltrate and discover what should not be possible, at least according to the standards of what most believe. It was this same nature of thinking and movement that allowed her to exist unnoticed among killers, thieves, and drug dealers, at least for a time. It was the ability to see information veiled to others and then use what most think to be weakness as the very strength that helped her overcome and conquer. Beatrix had been labeled from a young age, and that label took hold as the truth about Beatrix, but that was anything but the truth. Beatrix herself began to believe their narrative of her, even becoming hopeless and losing faith at times. But Beatrix had learned in the field of business, where she excelled, the necessity of just acting out the label assigned to her.

Now, she didn't act it out fully; just enough to fool those who were trying to fool her—or worse, harm her. She could morph into the character they defined her as being, and yet keep her integrity in tack. For her, it became a layer of armor, a tool needed for the job at hand. For those who mislabeled her, it turned out to be their weakness and undoing.

Beatrix understood danger well and could sniff it out quickly. She always knew when something wasn't right. She also had an accurate way of discovering the truth about others, determining their motives, and predicting their moves in advance. By just assuming the role of the character as they had labeled her, she disarmed her opponents, allowing her to move more freely and gain access beyond what her reach would otherwise have been. In business, Beatrix had learned to turn this into a challenging game, to keep positive while enduring the mistreatment that came with the label. She learned to see it as a challenge when peers or managers placed her within boundaries that she exceeded. Beatrix held a rare gift of knowing people better than they knew themselves, and this became a trump card in her hand, to which their underestimation blinded them.

Beatrix on Becoming the Label Assigned to You

This allows you to get an overall snapshot of strengths, weaknesses, and potential openings within a landscape. First, you must clear your mind of the garbage intake, noise and distractions meant to create an illusion or an altered reality and perception. Remember, start with a clean slate. Meaning, take all the information (lying in plain view on the tabletop) and dump it on the floor as the rubbish it is. Here are some guidelines:

1. Start with the characters who have no influence over the direction of the group. They may think they have influence,

but their perception of the situation is irrelevant to your gathering of truthful details.

2. Next, look for the characters who are trying to persuade others of their power and influence within the group.

The first two scans around the room will have cleared out most of the characters from the drawing board. Now you should be down to just a few remaining people. These are the people of most importance in your plan of approach. These are the people you need to gain a better understanding of. They hold the power to shift the direction of the group. Take your time in observing the group, understanding them, assessing their overall position and potential within the group. This process will not be easy or quick initially, especially if it's not a normal aspect of your mode of operation. To do this with accuracy, remember to make no assumptions and take no one's word about anything or anyone. You must do this work yourself, allowing no aid from anyone in your assessments. No one should even be aware of your process. It should be seamless and unnoticeable. The moment you allow influence over your assumptions, your work becomes clouded and inaccurate. To view accurately, you must observe with a neutral lens and have no emotion attached to your conclusions. You should observe people in the same way a scientist views subjects of study. This is just the first wave of discernment steps. You must remember to check your ego at the door before entering your lab as a "mad scientist"! As you repeat this process, it will make more sense to you. You will begin to see how all the moving parts, patterns, and exercises will combine for highly accurate discernment, critical Thinking, and decision-making. *Discern, decode, decide,* and then you can plan a correctly executed approach! You can apply this to all areas of life—personal, business, social, and even social media if that becomes a tool of discovery.

Beatrix's Important Clues for Sorting and Eliminating

Be aware of the following personalities and behaviors:

1. Loud attention-seekers
2. Busybodies/troublemakers
3. Regurgitators (no original thoughts, "he said/she said," or offering only clichés)
4. Passive-aggressives (no courage/cowardice)
5. Bosses of one and all (controllers)
6. Schmoozers/manipulators
7. Labelers (arrogance, ignorance, or both)
8. Gobblers (eat everything fed to them by controllers or surroundings; easy and usable targets)
9. People pleasers (fake nice types; can be bought easily)
10. Mighty morph power (*dangerous*—people with this ability can do what you do, at least at some level!)

Who's in the Sandbox?

Beatrix

So, after you have made the first wave of assessments, you must refine the process and troubleshoot any problems that may exist within your approach. You need to study patiently until you have a good feel for all the characters, but you must also plan for any unknowns. Remember, allow room for error! You must have a good understanding of who's in the room, or "sandbox," as I like to call it. Dealing with the various characters or personalities is very much like little kids playing in a sandbox. You've got the loud obnoxious kids, the quiet and shy kids, the floater kids who are so unsure of who they are, changing with each new friend they encounter. And, finally, the bullies throwing sand at everyone in the sandbox.

These are very general categories; however, most personalities will fall within a range somewhere in these subcategories. Your goal will be to sort through the characters quickly on the first scan, looking for the weakest characters, those lacking foundation and balance. These are the easiest characters to overcome and get past. They are basic floaters, with no real purpose or substance (sheep). Because they lack a solid foundation and sureness of themselves in authentic terms, they become easily moved and manipulated. This may sound bad, but, remember, if you are applying such a technique, it means that this team represents danger or harm to you or others. If you can't assess them properly, then you will be at their mercy and subject to the labels they assign to you. You must always keep strict measures of any techniques used against the foundational rules you have established for yourself. If you break your foundational rules, then you will suffer the consequence of that slipup. No team is ever better than the weakest members, so if you wish to keep your team safe and successful, you must not yield to weak tactics driven by emotions or prideful ego. This technique requires the utmost in integrity and care, as well as a humble attitude. You will be required to swallow your pride and take many punches for the team.

Can you think of times when you have watched others change or alter themselves according to the people they are with at the time? This can be a bad thing, or it can be quite the opposite: a good thing and, in fact, a strength. What defines which it is? That depends. Is it their standard mode of operating in order to achieve acceptance? Or, instead, is it a method of understanding the landscape and effectively managing the surroundings in order to survive? As we have seen, the former can become a problem, while the latter can be used as a tool to become a strength. So, what I mean is; What is their motive for behavior and/or actions? You cannot assume to know their true motives, so you will need to engage with them to learn more about their general character and underlying motives.

We have all seen the foregoing happen, and perhaps even done it ourselves. This can be a slippery slope, since we can become unauthentic, lose the respect of others, and then be viewed as unreliable. In the time I spent with Beatrix, she had found a rather genius way of using this as an effective tool—a strength—while remaining genuine and authentic. Beatrix had experienced inaccurate labels throughout her life. This was particularly frustrating for her, as she was generally underestimated. When she was young and immature, she told me of times that she attempted to convince those around her that she was qualified for more-challenging opportunities, or simply that she was different than they perceived or heard her to be. This was only met with jokes to brush her off, or with responses that reiterated the black-and-white ideas of educational, gender, or class limitations. As a result, the few corporate jobs she held were short-lived, suffocating, and miserable. She realized that her best opportunities would revolve around the sales profession or entrepreneurial ventures. She knew these fields would balance her performance and advancement opportunities in a fairer assessment. This alone didn't change the fact that she was labeled inaccurately, but it put her in charge of her destination.

Beatrix explained to me her most unusual process of dealing with those who labeled her. As mentioned, she learned to use the labelers to her advantage. She turned an oppressive, impossible situation into a chess game of sorts, overcoming their ignorance and eventually earning the respect and friendship of many who initially misjudged her. She had experimented enough with varying methods to understand that mere words spoken would never shift the thoughts of anyone. Whatever ideas or beliefs people hold, simply telling them something will never be enough to change or break those deeply ingrained thoughts. Rather, it's a complex and difficult task requiring patience, wisdom, and endurance. The disadvantages became transformed into advantages, in much the same way as Beatrix transformed herself into what was needed for the task at hand. Use what you have! Morph into what is needed!

Beatrix had been programmed for difficulty throughout her life, which seemed to assist her in moving to effective solutions quickly and before her opponents could notice. Defeat was never considered as an option on her menu board of choices. I know you may be thinking that Beatrix must have viewed many in her life negatively, but that couldn't be farther from the truth. Beatrix was like no one I'd ever known, a real mystery to solve. She often joked with me about her infamous nature: a real paradoxical enigma that could never quite fit into any box. She saw it as particularly amusing that she had to fight her way out of boxes when there was no box to categorize her rare persona.

CHAPTER 8

Move Like a Ninja

Before beginning any new movement, you may want to review the foundational rules of truth that you have established for yourself. When you begin to move in new and different ways, it will be a challenge for you, and it will also be challenging for those who know you. Those you know *will not* accept you stepping out of your rightful box! If you haven't built your strategy against truths that you can rely on, it will become the sabotage of your new movement. For, without this strategy in place, when you begin to feel the heat of change—and you most definitely will—you will inevitably fold under the pressure. Also, if you haven't carefully followed the steps outlined earlier, you may not have the strength to carry through. When the challenges of change come, you will become weakened, at least for a moment. However, if you have done the work bringing you to this point, you will stand strong! You will know and understand the change you are pursuing, and the strategy map necessary to get you there. You will have planned for obstacles and hardships. It's very likely that the opposition has noticed that you are about to make a transition. If they have noticed something, they've probably written it off, believing themselves to be impenetrable, or you too weak for the challenge. They likely believe you would never have the courage or wherewithal to challenge their systems. So, use their ignorance and ego as your advantage! They are not aware of the "new you" that is about to emerge. They aren't aware of how your change will even put them in a great position for positive changes. They don't know ... so, you must fully know and understand what you are doing, and *why*. They will only see it as negative or as something they must defeat. But, if you have done the work, gathering new tools needed for the war of change, they will not stop the change. Be prepared for battle, as you begin to transform into what will be required of you for the change you are seeking. And, believe it or not, through your transformation, even some who may be opponents now may also be moved to positive changes for themselves, propelled by the movement you create. When you move in a new way, they, too, are forced to move in new way. It begins with you, and new movement! Their decision will be if they themselves will grow in the opportunity of change, or, instead, find their own demise in holding on to the things that dictated your need to move differently. That should not be your focus; I am simply making you aware of the fact that those who oppose you today may advocate for new principles that you represent tomorrow. Change is a messy job, *not* for those unwilling to do the work, not for those unprepared to get bumps and bruises, and not for those who are weak at heart.

We each have a form of superhero within us. We can only connect to our power by embracing our true authentic selves. We cannot politely sit in the confined spaces we've been assigned. This task is very difficult because it will inevitably place you at odds with those who say you should be doing things according to their plan for your life, based on the assessment they have made of you. By continuing down this path, it becomes a form of worshipping another human, or for whatever strings we feel this person represents in our favor. In other words, we trade authentic self for this other version that pleases another person. Why? Think about what you fear about that person or what he or she represents to you, and you will find your conclusion or price so to speak. You probably believe that person holds the strings that will make or break you, or give you what you desire. Perhaps that person represents everything you've ever wanted. It will require some self-exploration for you to determine why you are willing to trade in your true self, and maybe even your beliefs, for an identity that doesn't belong to you. Discover the power, perceived or real, that the person holds over you, and then determine if that is worth giving up your authentic self and the life in store for you—the one that God has purposed just for you. There is no right or wrong answer here. Instead just the consequence or price you have determined to live with.

We have covered many steps that will assist you in new movement. It will take some time for it to feel comfortable. It's like any other change you may desire: new disciplines will have to be formed to integrate permanent changes. Prepare yourself for the completely awkward feeling of transforming yourself. It will even feel wrong to you at times, and that is when you will review your foundational rules and all the supporting data you have collected. If you did those things properly up front, you will have no trouble getting right back on track. You will understand the feelings to be temporary emotions that are representing fear from the past you. You will dismiss it all quickly, knowing you have done the work to get you to this point, and you will trust yourself to proceed ahead. For all intents and purposes, you will become unrecognizable, an unpredictable ninja for change!

Some of the most important things to be aware of and take precautions against are old emotions, attitudes, and ego from past self, all of which led you to the point of recognizing the change(s) you need to make. You will need to always be very consciously aware of your state of being and movements, which must now be dictated by decisively choosing new emotional responses, checking ego, and cultivating correct attitudes. If you want transformative change, you must approach it seriously, taking on the responsibility and pain of the cause. Find your power, and build a team whose members have powerful skills rooted in truth!

> The easiest men/women to take out of a room are the noisiest by nature, and those with the biggest egos in play.
>
> —MindScope Seven

Transform Emotions and Ego into Attitude and Discipline

What a paradoxical thought! I am telling you to have an attitude rather than gush emotions all over the place and act out your issues. I am talking about a correct attitude for the job or circumstances you are dealing with. A chosen attitude that you have derived carefully, based on all the data, characters, and circumstances in question. Choosing the correct attitude for each task of change is a method that becomes a tool you control, using it for the job and then slipping it back into your tool belt. The mistake most people make is having attitude based only on their emotions, and that destroys all productive solutions. This is not to say that at times the opposers will say you have an attitude. See this as a sign that you are doing it right! So, from this day forward, remember you will not yield to attitude; instead, you will become a changeable instrument used for directing change. Use attitude as a tool, and do not allow it to engulf you or get you off course. Remember, you chose it (proper attitude); never allow it to choose you (attitude based on emotions). This is nothing more than disciplined approach, but it requires practice and checking emotions and ego at the door. When you design your movement this way in business or in the difficult battle of change, your movements become like those of a ninja, and thereby completely unpredictable to those who may oppose you and your efforts. I always get into trouble with this one, because it seems cold to people when I first advise this technique. It is merely discipline being used to get the job done; *it is not who you are.* The important thing regarding attitude is that you stay in control and choose the attitude needed for the task at hand. Never allow your attitude to be an extension of what you are feeling (your emotional state). Again, you should choose your attitude based on the task at hand and the information collected. Think of your attitude as an interchangeable tool. Visualize it in your tool belt as a variety of different types of screwdrivers, and then match it to what the task is calling for. For instance, you could never use a Phillips-head screwdriver with a flat screw. It would never work. Not only would your efforts fail, but you would also have opened a door of opportunity for the adversary to walk right through, because you could not complete the task. A costly mistake, and your task just became more difficult because of your failure to assess properly. Never choose a tool based on what you are feeling! As you begin to experiment with these tried and proven methods, understand that correctly completing the task at hand is far more important than any people-pleasing method that might seem a lesser risk. Anything out of context or misused always goes awry. And that leads to the second part of this equation: trading ego for discipline. Most human beings get this completely opposite, and it precludes their success.

Let's begin with emotion. When you plug into emotion for any task, it's like getting into a bumper car and trying to guess where you will end up. It is completely uncertain, and you get banged up from every direction. It is not that emotions are a bad thing; it's just never the purpose of emotion to dictate strategic plans or actions. That always ends in disaster. Let me suggest a few simple rules to follow in regard to emotions:

1. Emotions are meant to be an alarm system.
2. Never act while under the influence of emotions; wait until emotions subside.

3. Emotions are meant for you to share with those you intimately love (close friends, family).

4. Emotions discolor truth and lead to delusions, making everything built around them unreliable.

5. Emotions are never your friend in strategic planning or business.

You are probably thinking, *Wow! What a cold way to approach life.* If so, that is because you misunderstand just how much emotions fling you around, keeping you confused and causing you to make bad decisions. I certainly feel emotions, but I have learned to carefully process them in my own time (think tank), not in the time of others. After I have processed their meaning (if any), I then go back to the drawing board. By doing this, you maximize the potential of your approach. The moment you lead with emotion, you lose, and so do those who rely on your decision-making ability. This is a foundational rule for me, and I strongly suggest you adopt this if you wish to change the success rate of your endeavors.

Imagine a typical moment when life thrusts something upon you, with no warning; it immediately sends you into a wave of overwhelming emotion, followed by a string of incorrect actions. Can you relate to this happening? It has probably guided you more frequently than you would ever admit. What should you do in that very moment? Here is where your foundational rules come into play. Figure out a systematic response when this happens. If necessary, *stop, drop,* and *roll.* Do whatever it takes to stop the emotions from overriding the brain. Make up any method for yourself necessary to force you into discipline mode, back to your list of foundational rules and your strategic plan. For me, in business, there were two main rules that always assisted my stoppage. As soon as I would feel the onset of the emotions, justified or not, I would give myself a time-out period. I would then refer to my foundational rules, the first two being:

1. My emotions are reserved for those I love and am intimately connected to.
2. I will do nothing until all emotion subsides, and I have a clear head for strategizing and planning.

This has always been enough for my redirection, but you must build a system that works for you. Doing the above has always offered me a cooling-off and reflective period. I would take the time that I needed until I knew for certain that all emotion had been tabled effectively and that I had a well-thought-out plan of action. Most times, after review of the bigger picture and risk weighed against possible reward, I would decide to do absolutely nothing. This does not mean that emotions are not justified; rather, it affirms that they usually create disruption and destruction, and rarely anything productive.

Allowing emotions to drive the car to your destination is like a parent sitting in the backseat of a car and allowing their underage, unlicensed, immature child to drive the car. A recipe for disaster. Instead, take your emotions to a healthy place for you to unload and process (think tank). Maybe this is at the gym, or perhaps a private place of solitude. It can be wherever and whatever works for you; just not out in the open.

Ego works very much the same as emotion in terms of the disciplines needed to adjust for productive living and change. However, ego is a bit more complex in terms of what creates an immature or out-of-check ego. Much like emotions, ego becomes a very destructive force when it's in control of you. Since ego takes a bit of time to unravel, for the sake of moving forward toward change, just assume as a rule to check ego at the start of the task. Instead, only rely on what the data you collected points to. So often, ego is built on perception only, rarely on logic, truth, or reality.

Ego, too, can be a destroyer of success, not just limited to business but also to far greater problems within family and self. How many times have we seen the story repeat itself of highly successful people falling off the wagon? The problem that brings them to this point is an out-of-check ego. They begin to believe themselves to be untouchable, more than they are, and above others around them. This notion is bound for failure, and they often lose everything important to them. They have assumed the role that the ego dictates, completely detaching from authentic self, and therefore incapable of productive actions that will ensure a balanced life and future success. We often see those with out-of-check egos in positions of power and leadership; however, rarely does that combination turn out well for them or those they serve.

> For by the grace given me I say to every one of you:
> Do not think of yourself more highly than you ought,
> but rather think of yourself with sober judgment,
> in accordance with the faith God has distributed
> to each of you. in accordance with the faith God
> has members do not all have the same function,
> so in Christ we, though many, form one body, and
> each member belongs to all the others. We have
> different gifts, according to the grace given to each
> of us. If your gift is prophesying, then prophesy
> in accordance with your faith; if it is serving,
> then serve; if it is teaching, then teach; if it is to
> encourage, then give encouragement; if it is giving,
> then give generously; if it is to lead, do it diligently;
> if it is to show mercy, do it cheerfully.
>
> —Romans 12:3–8 (NIV)

You must consciously keep putting yourself back on the mark of consciousness, so to speak, especially when enjoying success. To keep the ego in a balanced position involves a continuous placing of yourself in the proper light regarding the good of humankind and the motives within your heart. We always exist in two realities (internal and external) at the same time, and this often results in a misguided ego. There is an existence that society creates and beckons us to join by developing an overinflated ego, creating a selfish and self-serving platform. All sorts of ugliness, hatred, abuse, a variety of self-indulgent behaviors, and even crime emerge from this platform. This platform may rise quickly, holding power and prestige, but, eventually, it leads to problems and a tumbling fall. An ego that grows wildly out of balance leads its owner to weakness, all the while entrancing him or her into believing in the falsehood of strength and power that ego lures them into believing are truth. They begin to believe in the noise around them, the definitions applied to them by strangers, and so they become legends in their own minds.

Furthermore, this becomes a door of entry for adversaries to take over the kingdom, and you will never even see the onset of adversaries. They won't have to hide anything, because you've become so blind to the "truth" the gigantic ego keeps whispering in your ear. It is wise to develop foundational rules for yourself to guard against this sneaky attacker. I've always had a built-in signaling system for myself, and a disciplined process I would take myself through, in order to place myself back on the narrow line needed to have continued success, along with actions that would provide good and responsible service for those I served. Remember, we are to serve, not be served! In my own process, my mind would engage quietly, often, and repeatedly in order to ward off this ugly beast.

Summary of Key Foundational Rules

1. Never believe in, or become, the noise about you or around you.

2. If people (male or female) are overly critical or overly complimentary, watch out: they are attempting to change your balance and stroke your ego. This is never good, so dismiss it completely!

3. There is always someone bigger, better, stronger, or smarter than you are. That person is forever in pursuit of taking your lunch, so push yourself for growth. Don't allow anyone to take your lunch through the weakness and lies ego whispers in your ear. This equates to you "giving your lunch" freely to the adversary wishing to snatch it. Easy backdoor entry! *Close all doors*, through constant preparedness.

4. Understand the value of others around you in comparison to your talents and abilities; assess what everyone brings to the table, including you. Basically, this is a recognition of your humble contribution as a member of the team—or just one of humankind. Do not take on pride or think your role to be overly important or irreplaceable. We are all replaceable!

The last point is so important, it bears repeating: *We are all replaceable.* In addition, we invite our replacement through our overinflated egos, unchecked emotions, lack of discipline, and incorrect attitudes, all of which lead us to fail to complete our principal task in the broader perspective, beyond ourselves. We each are but a paid, temporary, or replaceable resource. Our correct view of our own position dictates our necessity, longevity, and trustworthiness to enhance and complete any task.

And then, there is the bigger reality, of recognizing our place as individual members of the greater body of humankind, providing a variety of functions as a contribution to humankind's betterment, not just a selfish platform for our own advancement. This leads to another leg of the emotion control game. And that is, What happens when you are stuck for a period in the middle of some emotional quagmire where darts and bullets are flying all around your head, and you must stay for a prolonged period? Then what? I always made it a practice in business to never allow anyone in the room to measure me, what I was thinking or feeling. The best way to do this, is to know how to wear a poker face. Never allow others to read you!

Poker Face versus Intimacy

In business, or in any battle you may face, it is imperative that you remain a mystery, and ever changing. This is not for the purpose of fooling others, but, rather, for the more important purpose of correctly discerning our environment and maintaining safety for ourselves and those relying on our efforts. This might mean our own families, our communities, or our jobs. Although we might find ourselves in unjust systems beyond our control, we must find ways to exists peacefully and still be able to succeed.

You must set your own standard to hold your ground and operate in a mode consistent with your foundational rules. This can become rather difficult in professional settings. If you aren't prepared with a plan, you will be moving at the mercy of *their* plan, perhaps lacking integrity. In most cases, their plan will require you to alter your own standards and, thereby, your integrity. We certainly can't go into a professional organization and attempt to change it to meet our own requirements. That's equally as ridiculous as casting your standards to the wind, and trading them for prestige, popularity, or position. This doesn't mean that positive change can't happen over time, but that will be unknown initially. We must exist and work peacefully with others while holding our character and integrity true to form, true to our own foundational rules.

Let's consider a simple example of what this might look like in everyday life. When you are in the team environment at work, and everyone is dying laughing about some joke a team member just shared, you might ignore it completely, as if you didn't even hear it. Other times, you might choose to laugh. The object is to be unreadable—leave people guessing as to what your response will be—so that no one will accurately assess your thoughts, opinions, or movement.

In other words, just allow them to believe in whatever label that they assigned you. This can be a very useful tactic, especially while you are actively assessing the characters in the room. You want to be under the radar, seen as no threat, so as to keep their interest off you—or even have them underestimate you completely.

Another example might be when someone in the group is stirring a pot of conflict. You play it cool and ignore it or redirect the energy and remove yourself; but, no matter what, do not give in or join them. When you are working under the radar and enacting their label of you, stay true to your foundational rules and integrity. You must strictly adhere to your foundational rules at all times, no matter what mask you might temporarily wear for the cause. Basically, if they label you, allow it; live it out to the fullest, within the boundaries of integrity and authenticity.

Remember, a group will always label you and others in the environment. Most will eventually begin to live out the negativity of the label, but you choose to use the label effectively for good cause.

Beatrix on Being the Underdog

I have often found myself in the underdog position. I found out quickly that the more your resist it or attempt to convince them otherwise, the more difficulty, even danger, it creates for you. You may say that I learned to turn lemons into lemonade. A visual and narrative that I created to hold my authentic self to the line and not submit to their actions of weakness was this: *Hah! You will regret this.* I then visualized how I would use their bad treatment of me to create the catapult for good or change. I learned to use it like a game in my mind. This kept me in a positive state mentally and relaxed in whatever I was encountering daily in their mistreatment. I understood their actions to be coming from a place of weakness, and I realized that as long as I did no harm and stuck to my own rules and integrity, all would be well. I knew I could not lose if I kept my standards and motives correct, even if my choice became to leave. Whenever you are in a position of being abused or mistreated, you have to find another way to plug your energy into the process so that you stay positive, clearheaded, calm, and on task. This turns your position of underdog into a position of empowerment, and then you just allow them to play out their little evil plots, within reason. You can then take over control of the trajectory; or, you can abort the mission, and leave. Just trust yourself in making the right decision, if you are utilizing the correct tools for discernment. They never even realize what's happening, because they are so inundated with their own ill intents and motives. It requires much patience to work through the difficulty, but it is an opportunity to learn to enjoy the challenge of fighting evil with good. If you assess it's a worthwhile project for your overall goal, the temporary difficulties are just bumps between you and the difference that is needed.

Keeping the poker-face demeanor creates confusion amongst those opposing you or change. It also keeps you in charge of your response rather than flowing with the weaker response of the crowd. There will be times when you'll choose to respond in a certain way for the sake of the cause, not because of your emotions. This doesn't mean you never smile or show expression. It means you choose what they see, by design, and never allow them to know your ideas, feelings, or emotions from authentic self. Remember, revealing your authentic self is a privilege shared with those you trust and love in intimate relationships and close friendships.

So, What about Intimacy?

Intimacy holds itself to a small reserved space, only for those who have earned trust and then consistently act in ways that represent your best interest and safety. Even within that small space, the segmentation can be even more refined. Let me explain this further. Let's say you have two very dear friends who both fit the qualifications of intimacy; however, one friend is someone you go to more for business issues, while the other is more of resource in personal matters. You would still have defined boundaries between these friends because you would not necessarily trust them with the same information.

To simplify this to an easier daily operation, consider that you hold three circles around you. Most people you encounter are within the farthermost outer circle. These tend to be casual acquaintances; even if you see them often, that does not earn them a spot in one of the inner circles. The middle circle is reserved for casual friends, with a different set of established boundaries that you keep. They don't need to know your established rules; these are implied by your interactions with them. You reserve the right to move people to different circles at any time you deem necessary. Have a clear understanding of your own criteria of the difference between casual acquaintance and casual friend.

Now to the innermost circle. This is a strongly guarded place to which few ever find the door of entry. These are people who, over a course of time and events, have offered you enough supporting evidence to prove their trustworthiness and loyalty. Most of us would be lucky to have five close friends, along with some family members, in this circle. Even family members do not get automatic access to this circle. This inner circle is the most intimate and revealing place, where we can safely be ourselves without fearing judgment or backlash. It is a place of refuge and strength, with a few people who have integrated their lives in such a way that they can usually predict the thoughts and actions of one another with fair accuracy.

Intimacy is a critical element of our lives, but most never experience it or execute it properly. It is a yearning built within us, which, when not attended to, gets confused with other things. We live in a society that encourages oversharing and a pretense of sameness, which not only is *not* true but also causes a variety of problems. Society likes to label people as *strange* or *loners* if they choose to live a life with reasonable boundaries in place. Establishing boundaries does not mean that you don't like others; it simply indicates an issue of compatibility and shared similar values. We should be able to work and coexist with all people peacefully, but that does not mean everyone gets access to our intimate space. This is neither good or bad; it is neutral regarding our interaction with others. It also allows individuals to live with more clarity and peace around them, making them able to thrive in all types of relationships and creating a domino effect of good all around.

The biggest problem with intimacy issues tends to show up as something like this: Time at home with the family (meaning, spouse and children) becomes distant, a mere going through the motions, until there are no meaningful connections. And then the people at work getting the best of what you have to offer; you spend more time there, even problem solving with people who may be completely absent from your life in a matter of days or months. Basically, you are giving your best to strangers, taking the leftovers home to your family, the very people you are responsible for and will likely be at your bedside upon illness and death. This reverse order is killing our families, and that is spilling over in our communities—and the world. Spouses have little to no intimate connection, gravitating toward an us-against-them mentality, as men put their wives down around their friends, and then women do the same to their husbands with their female friends. This creates combative relationships, with little trust, and, most often, end in divorce. The children suffer the loss of intimate connection with one or both parents. Many are growing up in one-parent homes; or, perhaps, both parents are physically present but totally unavailable for their children. Intimacy is critically important to the structure and health of our families and outer communities. It holds critical keys to the emotional well-being of all people, and the lack thereof creates far-reaching problems that we all must cope with.

Family Structure

Although two-parent families are becoming less common in many parts of the world, they still constitute a majority of families around the globe. Children are particularly likely to live in two-parent families in Asia and the Middle East, compared with other regions of the world. Children are more likely to live with one or no parent in the Americas, Europe, Oceania, and sub-Saharan Africa than in other regions. Extended families (which include parent[s] and kin from outside the nuclear family) also appear to be common in Asia, the Middle East, Central/South America, and sub-Saharan Africa, but not other regions of the world.

Marriage rates are declining in many regions. Adults are most likely to be married in Asia and the Middle East, and are least likely to be married in Central/South America, with Africa, Europe, North America, and Oceania falling in between. Cohabitation (living together without marriage) is more common among couples in Europe, North America, Oceania, and, especially, in Central/South America.

The nature, function, and firsthand experience of marriage vary around the world. Marriage looks and feels different in Sweden as compared with the experience in Saudi Arabia; in China, compared with the experience in Canada; and in Argentina, compared with the experience in Australia; and so on. Nevertheless, across time and space, in most societies and cultures, marriage has been an important institution for structuring adult intimate relationships and connecting parents to one another and to any children that they have together. In particular, in many countries, marriage has played an important role in providing a stable context for bearing and rearing children, and for integrating fathers into the lives of their children.

Intimacy is one of the most difficult emotions for human beings to connect to, because they fear the vulnerability that it brings. However, without intimacy, we become starved and unbalanced. If a relationship become starved of this key ingredient, it usually finds its expiration date. People fear intimacy because something inside them is not whole; they fear that through intimacy weakness may be revealed. They use all sorts of excuses about intimacy. They try to replace it with all types of other things. In example, Guys may say, "She is not going to tell me what to do" and Women use intimacy as a weapon.

These are just a few toxic thoughts and examples played out in personal relationships. It goes further, though, bleeding into every relationship a person has and eventually making all of them superficial and at risk. As less intimacy occurs, the focus shifts to winning or one-upping the other person. This is just the beginning of the downhill slide of human relations lacking intimacy. By replacing intimacy with superficial interactions, all else in the relationship becomes tainted. Could a void of healthy intimate connections offer us some clues on what is happening to family structure and stability throughout our communities and the world?

Our minds are powerful, and when we allow our thoughts to plug into wrong information, it begins to alter our behaviors in ways that are counterproductive to the outcomes we hoped for. Even in relationships where one partner is approaching intimacy correctly, if the other isn't, the relationship still becomes dysfunctional. One person working authentically cannot overcome the damage of the other person operating in unauthentic ways. Intimacy places us in a raw, vulnerable position, usually creating uncomfortable emotions. Oftentimes fear sets in feeding our minds with inaccurate information. We become convinced of what our emotions are feeding us, and then we believe intimacy to be the wrong approach. So, to be certain, we talk over the misinformation with our friends, and they are more than willing to back us up on the trick of our emotions. This offers us even more excuses and support to enable bad behavior. We begin applying tactics of war to our families, our community, and our world, and then we wonder what's wrong. Can you see the problems that have festered from this misapplied thinking? Strategic moves, mind games, passive-aggressive behaviors, harsh words and treatment, and the like are *meant for war!* Could this be a clue as to the brother-against-brother mentality that we are living out in our families behind closed doors, and in our community in the streets? How can any family or society survive, much less thrive, when we are operating in this mind-set?

Intimacy means to show up *authentically* in all aspects of relating. And then, to hold the proper alignment of intimacy within the three circles of security around you and your family. When you find that you are dealing with an individual who refuses to operate with integrity or authenticity, your success will be limited, tiresome, and lacking satisfaction. It begins with each person on the individual level. It may be helpful to begin thinking about what you are afraid of in terms of relating. There are definite differences in how we relate in different types of relationships, and how much we may share. However, the common thread to all types of relationships is that to live peacefully and function at the highest level of performance must begin with the basics of intimacy and authenticity. Remember this final thought as you begin to explore in your own mind: it is the strong man or woman who lives life authentically through intimately relating to others in appropriate ways. Such individuals give of themselves and serve their families, communities, and workplaces in an honest fashion. Intimacy is a critical key to living successfully! We will never know another person until we give our time and attention to understanding him or her. We should spend our energy getting to know a person, rather than judging from afar or basing our opinion on secondhand gossip. Doing this alone would solve many problems.

Strengths Equal Weakness

Our strengths can equally become our biggest weakness, when applied incorrectly. We have seen how Beatrix was able to take her weaknesses and transform them into strengths to conquer. She could succeed at this because she knew herself so well. She had a clear understanding of her authentic self, but she was constantly seeking to prove herself wrong, finding the error of her own actions. She understood that if those errors weren't extracted and resolved, it would leave the door open for the opposition to walk through and conquer any plan of action she had determined.

This relentless pursuit of growing beyond the present forced the acceptance of new challenges. Whereas most of us avoid the unknown, Beatrix was drawn to what she had not yet learned. She had a clear understanding, when acting, that the very strengths she possessed could blow up in her face if she neglected to carefully apply her knowledge and understanding of the other characters. So, as she was making determinations, she was also careful to build into her system of thought and approach a counterbalance that would act as a preventive measure for not allowing strengths to become destructive weaknesses.

Exercise

1. List what you believe your greatest strengths to be, and then describe how that may be applied in transforming you or your team's outcome in overcoming obstacles.
2. Now think about those strengths in reverse. How could they become the demise of yourself and the others in your care?
3. List what you believe to be your weaknesses or, perhaps, mislabels you have received. Explain in detail the barriers that these cause, and also how they negatively impact your relations with others.

CHAPTER 9

Refuel Your Mission

In all the conversations I had with Beatrix, the one action she repeatedly relied on to refuel her mission was prayer. Early in life, with all around her that was outside her control, Beatrix learned that it was necessary to rely on a Higher Power.

She expressed that her prayer life had drastically changed during the period of more than five years when she faced full out war in her world. During this time, she explained that she prayed all day long on many occasions. She was still going about her daily life, but the prayers persisted throughout her day in all she did. She knew that prayer kept her focused and calm, enabling her to deal with the dangers and problems she had to face. She further explained the remarkable difference in her experience of prayer at that time: it was more than just the frequency; it was also a deeply personal and intimate connection between her and God. She continually used the word *intimacy* to describe the experience. She said that, for the first time in her life, she felt a true connection to a Higher Power. She had always served God, but He seemed out of her reach, and she felt she was not that important to Him—not ever good enough for Him.

Looking back now, she has come to understand how that impaired her spiritual life. She was great at following the rules of her beliefs, but she never felt love from God. She now knows that wasn't true, and attributes her feelings to what she always knew to be a problem: a misunderstanding of God through the teaching and environments into which she was forced. She had already been working on this spiritual connection for more than a decade when the war found her doorstep. She had already made the necessary steps in detaching from environments that had used God inappropriately and caused harm and confusion.

Consequently, during the most-difficult challenges and dangers she ever faced, she had found this completely different level of connection with God. A level where she had access to tools that He provided her, allowing her to overcome things that she never could have surmounted on her own. She had a new closeness with God, an intimacy she described as akin to talking to a best friend, but with the proper reverence and honor owed Him. Her accounts of the experiences she had with God during this time were at once overwhelming and miraculous. I want to emphasize how much she now desires that others understand how she obtained this. This changed everything for her and gave her complete trust in God, because as she followed the unclear path He insisted she take, He protected her. And then, only after she obeyed completely, He revealed the *why*. She still feels a certain level of unbelief regarding the circumstances He guided her through, in terms of the reality that she did actually survive. Nevertheless, all she did was walk in swift, unquestioning obedience, in faith that He would take care of the rest. There were many times when Beatrix thought that day would be her last, but through His mercy and grace, she was spared. As Beatrix recalled the many things she experienced, she was rarely able to talk about it without tears—tears not of sadness but of joy in what she discovered. She expressed it to me in this way: "I want everyone to know about this power within their reach and access;

it will change everything for them. They just have to find the will to walk in the way of obedience and faith and be okay with the outcome He has for them, whatever it might be. I never knew that you could negotiate with God, but I did it; it required much from me, and it was well worth it. He can be trusted. I learned firsthand that He can be trusted!"

> I have fought the good fight, I have finished the race, I have kept the faith. Henceforth there is laid up for me the crown of righteousness, which the Lord, the righteous judge, will award to me on that day, and not only to me but also to all who have loved his appearing.
>
> —2 Timothy 4:7–8 (ESV)

Beatrix experienced much weariness, confusion, and even illness, just as any wounded warrior may endure in the heat of the battle. It is important to formulate a plan of how to refuel for the mission's completion; otherwise, you might be overwhelmed by the forces of the enemy. I asked Beatrix to recall a few of the most-difficult moments, the times when she truly felt that she might not survive. Below is a list of the tools she used most frequently in healing her wounds and restoring herself as the superhero warrior she was required to be in order to survive:

Superhero Tools for Survival

1. **Engage in continuous prayerful conversation with God.** (This will establish an intimate connection with Him, much like Beatrix experienced.)
2. **Create meditative quiet states so that you can hear the voice of God.** (This further will reinforce your intimate connection with Him, just as it did for Beatrix.)

3. **Spend time in your think tank.** (This was usually where Beatrix had the best conversation time with God, discussing things she was unsure of in terms of an approach He would be pleased with. This was a regular part of her routine, and she spent great amounts of time there. Her favorite think-tank venues were the gym, the garden, and anywhere that she could listen to the music of her choice.)

4. **Cultivate activities that connect your mind to your task/goal.** (Beatrix did this in regard to the war she faced. She began watching more documentaries regarding war. She had always been a fan of these, but at that time, when she felt weak or tired, watching these was like plugging into an energy source that renewed her mind for committing to the task ahead of her. She also became an avid fan of UFC[Ultimate Fighting Championship], because it put her in the mental state she had to be in [not her normal state of being] to deal with the characters she faced.)

5. **Accept your limits and know when it's time to rest and recharge.** (Beatrix learned to accept the days when she had nothing left to give, and then she retreated for the rest she needed in order to continue. "Wait until tomorrow" became her mantra, and tomorrow was always a renewed day for battle.)

6. **Learn to take the punches that come and do so with the grace God will give you.** (Beatrix learned to take those punches, "eating them," as she termed it, with the grace that only God could have given. Her mantra for this became "Eat it," and she learned to never flinch in the face of the enemy. She didn't need to, because she was wearing her armor.)

7. **Improve your ability to avoid wounds in battle.** (Beatrix became much better at avoiding battle wounds. She learned how to use the bait and traps set up by the opposition to trip or harm her. She prayed for God to reveal the enemy's

advances and to protect her if she became to weary to see them. She used everything thrown at her as another tool to defeat the enemy.)

8. **Never stop during battle.** (Beatrix never stopped, even when wounded; she remained determined to see it through, committed to crawling to her death if need be. Stopping in her battle would never be acceptable. She learned to crawl when necessary, but she never stopped.)

9. **Find teammates to renew and restore you.** (Beatrix found new teammates to help renew her when weariness overtook her, and to restore her hope so that she could finish the battle. She chose the people she knew had specific tools to help her in those moments. She understood her own weaknesses and wounds and framed her choices of teammates around them, choosing the people she believed in and trusted to share parts of her journey and help her refuel.)

10. **Fight!** (Beatrix certainly fought! When the wagon circlers sent in the opposition to stop her quest, she learned to fight in new and varied ways—as many as required. She molded herself into whatever the challenge called for, with a fight-or-die mentality. She fought hard, often taking on every person who decided to oppose her. By the grace of God, *she survived.*)

Analogy of an Athlete, from the Bible

Do you not know that in a race all the runners run, but only one receives the prize? So run that you may obtain it. Every athlete exercises self-control in all things. They do it to receive a perishable wreath, but we are imperishable. So I do not run aimlessly; I do not box as one beating the air. But I discipline my

body and keep it under control, lest after preaching
to others I myself should be disqualified.
                    —1 Corinthians 9:24–27 (ESV)

Paul uses runners in the Greek games as examples of how we are
to live as Christians. The first thing to notice is the utmost tension,
energy, and strenuous effort pictured by athletes straining for the
finish line in hope of the glory of winning. "This is the way to run,"
says Paul, "if we want to attain our potential."

This requires the steady, intense concentration or focus of the
runners. They cannot afford to become distracted by things off to
the side of their course. If they do, their effectiveness in running will
surely diminish. Keeping focused requires control—not allowing
distractions to interfere with the responsibility at hand. "Seek first
the kingdom of God and His righteousness," says Jesus (Matthew
6:33). Here, the issue is single-mindedness. James writes, "[H]e who
doubts is like a wave of the sea driven and tossed by the wind. ...
[H]e is a double-minded man, unstable in all his ways" (James 1:6,
8). Controlling our focus can go a long way toward making the run
successful.

Paul then says that the victorious runner sets Christians an example
of rigid self-control: "Everyone who competes for the prize is
temperate in all things [1 Corinthians 9:25 NKJV]." It is not only
a matter of concentrating while racing, but also in all areas of
life, because the runner's whole life impacts the race. The runner
religiously follows a rigorous program within a rigid schedule each
day: rising at a certain hour, eating a breakfast of certain foods,
filling the morning with exercises, and working on technique.
After a planned lunch, the runner continues training, eats a third
planned meal, and goes to bed at a specified hour. Throughout, the
runner not only avoids sensuous indulgences but must also abstain
from many perfectly legitimate things that simply do not fit into

the program. An athlete who is serious about excelling in a chosen sport must live this way; otherwise, he or she will not succeed except against inferior competitors. The undisciplined athlete will suffer defeat by those who do follow regimented programs.

We can learn a great deal here about self-indulgence and self-control. It is not enough for us to say, "I draw the line there, at this or that vice, and I will have nothing to do with these." We will have a very difficult time growing under such an approach, as Paul shows in Hebrews 12:1: "Therefore, we also since we are surrounded by so great a cloud of witnesses, let us lay aside every weight, and the sin which so easily ensnares us, and let us run with endurance the race that is set before us."

Many things that are not sinful are nevertheless "weights" simply because they are so time- and mind-consuming. Because we do not want to fail in accomplishing the highest purposes for which we were called, we must travel light while we run, in order to endure the length of our course successfully.

On the surface, it appears easy to be a Christian, inasmuch as a Christian is basically a person who trusts in Jesus Christ. No one is worthier of our trust, and He is fully able to bring us into the kingdom of God. But this is a mere surface observation. The truth is that being a Christian can be very difficult, because *true* Christians are those who, because they trust Christ, must set their heels upon the human nature within them and subordinate the appetites of the flesh and the desires of the mind, all with the ultimate aim of pleasing Him. No wishy-washy, irresolute, vacillating, lukewarm, disorderly, and/or unrestrained Christian will please our Master and glorify our Father.

Jesus says, "[N]arrow is the gate and difficult is the way which leads to life, and there are few who find it" (Matthew 7:14). Paul writes, "You therefore must endure hardship as a good soldier of Jesus Christ. No one engaged in warfare entangles himself with the affairs of this life, that he may please him who enlisted him as a soldier" (2 Timothy 2:3–4). Christians are exhorted to control themselves and run to win.

In 1 Corinthians, chapter 9, Paul illustrates self-control in its positive aspects by showing what it produces along the way and—most importantly—in the end. Jesus makes it clear in Revelation, chapters 2 and 3, that the overcomers (conquerors, victors) will go into the kingdom of God. Self-control plays a major role in bringing victory through our trusting relationship with Jesus Christ.

Andrew MacLaren, a Protestant commentator, states, "There are few things more lacking in the average Christian life of today than resolute, conscious concentration upon an aim which is clearly and always before us." Self-control is not the only factor we need to do this, but it is a very necessary one. Its fruit, good beyond measure, is worth every effort and sacrifice we must make.

Chapter 10

Superpowers Unleashed

Conclusions

Thank you for taking this wonderful journey of discovery in finding your own power and purpose. It's been a soulful journey to offer this gift; my hope is that some little morsel will make a powerful difference in your own life and the lives of others you encounter. It is so easy to read a book, store it away, and go back to business as usual. I hope you will keep this book handy as a reference guide to daily and major life choices. Hopefully, you will begin putting some of these concepts into practice before the bigger "thing/event" visits your life. What is practiced now will become second nature later, just as it was for Beatrix. She used her skills throughout her life, always further developing them into refined tools. When her bigger things began unfolding, she was ready to snap into action.

Most of us will never find ourselves facing the sorts of things that Beatrix did, and yet, some will face far worse. Life never delivers more than we are capable of handling, but our inner strength and voice may still have been dampened or lessened. I hope you, too, make the connection to the unending power and purpose within you. But what if you don't? What if you place this book in the pile of other books you own? What if you use it under the leg of a wobbly table? Will the things that drove you to purchase this book and then read it to completion suddenly disappear? We both know that isn't likely to happen. So, let's recap what you have gained, and then set a strategic plan for implementing the new tools, combined with approaches that will ensure your success.

In chapters 1 to 3, we began assessing the present-day problems of Beatrix, tracing them back to their root of origin. In this observation we could clearly see the connection between what began in her early years as a child and what was haunting her in the present, as we followed her to the bedside of her dying mother. That was a point of regret for Beatrix in terms of the way things had turned out for her mother and her siblings. It became such a life-altering event for Beatrix that she began a new journey, seeking to extract all that had so negatively impacted her, her mother, and the overall family unit. This was a time of undoing for Beatrix. A time that she wasn't sure she would survive, and then all those whom she and her mother had sacrificed so much for turned their backs on her. It became a moment of complete devastation for Beatrix, the thought that all their lives had been taken away to a large degree for no good purpose. Everything came into question for her at that time, and she felt so much anger for the falsehoods and lack of being able to live authentically.

So, I ask, Can you really afford to *not* take the opportunity to begin living your own life as your authentic self? Don't you and all those you cherish deserve the real you? This is the you so full of divine power, purpose, and potential. You may seem unrecognizable to many. The you that begins to advocate for self, assume the right to be the person you were designed to be and operate in alignment with your divine purpose.

Take time now to write a summary of where you are, as opposed to where you feel purposefully aligned. Writing it out serves as a commitment to yourself, as well as a report card for your progress as you begin to alter your destination.

You have already made your superhero foundational rules, so perhaps you can place them on a template the size of a credit card, which you can carry with you daily for easy access when you most need the rules. You could include your superhero tool belt on the opposite side, as a reminder of the weaponry you carry on board.

So, what if we took a different approach to the problems we face today in our families, our communities, and the world? What if we no longer viewed some as bad and others as good? What if we viewed our own responsibility in the equation of change, good over evil, by applying our unique talents and abilities as purposed? Can we absorb the powerful lessons from Beatrix, in a battle begun within family and culture, then ending up in the streets of her community in ways she had never imagined? Can many of the negatives we suffer in our world be tied to similar problems within our own cultural backgrounds? And, are we willing to address ourselves first as individuals, and then offer others in our communities the support needed in overcoming together? If we choose to remain complacent, what may come next? Allow your mind to explore varying possibilities. Use the tools provided to understand the strategic moves needed to preserve our families and communities from further deterioration.

Beatrix

I understand it now. The initial problem led me to the *real* fight: a war! This war was incomprehensibly bigger than me, bigger than all of us. God required me to walk in unknown enemy-filled territory. I still have difficulty believing this ever could have happened to me.

Everyone needs to know this: What God revealed to me through a dangerous series of terrifying events is proof we all can trust Him. It is only because of God (and those He sent to help me) that I am alive to tell you this story. The details I've already shared bear repeating here. When I set out on the lonely journey, I promised Him that I would do exactly what he told me, without question, and I did just that. If He would spare my son, I would go all in on whatever He asked of me; this was the deal I made with Him. I had lost my mother, I couldn't lose my son too—we had been through so much. But I *was* losing my son, to the streets, to addiction, to all the characters who control such things.

Oh God! I kept crying. I lay on my face, weeping, until He finally answered, saying he would restore my son, but He needed me to do this thing. This thing that I knew would be riddled with danger and might take my life. I made the deal. I never knew it was possible to make a deal with God. The terms of the deal didn't matter. I had no choice but to make the deal, because if I had to live after losing my son, I wouldn't really have a life at all. I walked in complete obedience, reliance, and faith that His promise of restoring my son would be kept, if I kept my promise to Him. I kept reminding Him, and He kept reminding me. This was my motivator for facing every fear, every challenge, every attempt on my own life. I could not fail in this task.

After a while, I realized there were others at risk; it wasn't just about my son anymore. I often thought, *God, what are You are thinking? I am not capable of this!* But then, I would remember His promise of not giving us more than our capabilities can handle. Without Him beside me, I could never have survived or done the things I did, which I couldn't even believe were happening. How could it be so? God can be trusted, and what I learned about Him through all of this is simple: it is all worth it. I want everyone to know this. It changed everything; He changed everything!

Thoughts and ideas (both good and bad) just like trees in the forest become deep-rooted systems within our families, community, and world. At one time they were just tiny seeds scattered around. Some washed away, never having an opportunity to develop. Others took root, and then systematically formed a very complex and strong root system, traveling to great depths and widths. Imagine how much force it might take to extract such an old and deeply rooted tree. This is exemplary of the similar daunting task of uprooting old thinking that no longer serves growth or sustains life. When we see growth hindered and life at risk, we must source the root of the problem. Then, we can begin the careful extraction process so that it is possible to revive life and thrive again. Just as it took years to build the deep-rooted system, it will also take time to find a cure for the ailments within our families and society. If we possess a solid foundation of mature, and developed growth on correct principals, the pruning process will be more successful. During the pruning process we must take care not to destroy the life source of the tree or humankind. But we must get started and be patient during the process of pruning and healing. By bringing to the table our united efforts, talents and gifts, we will be better able to serve the needs of the tree that serves us all with shade and shelter. We must pursue with the same level of patience and understanding as the time it took to create the deep-rooted system. We are all connected and responsible for maintaining the tree of life, necessary for the survival of humankind.

If ever I need to reach the root of a matter, or find courage to face a challenge, all I need do is call on my friend Beatrix. She has displayed her talents and abilities in use for the greater good, not of self but of others. I often recount her stories of how she found both superpower and purpose beyond what she had at a time, when all had abandoned her, leaving her to be devoured of wolves. But God had not left Beatrix, and it was because of this deeply intimate connection that she was able to survive. Through Beatrix I learned that we only need to seek, be swift in obedience, and walk in faith, even in times when we are outnumbered and surrounded by dark forces wishing to destroy us. I pray each day for Beatrix, that peace and healing will be restored to her; and I pray the same for all who are suffering the atrocities of this world. We must never lose hope, and we must remember that through God, *all things are possible!* We must determine to put on the armor of God ourselves, to be ever ready, better prepared, and ever willing to fiercely stand down the forces of dark power.

"Don't throw the baby out with the bathwater is an idiomatic expression for an avoidable error in which something good is eliminated when trying to get rid of something bad, or in other words, rejecting the favorable along with the unfavorable." German Proverb

"So that you may be sons of your Father who is in Heaven; for He causes His sun to rise on the evil and the good, and sends rain on the righteous and the unrighteous."—Matthew 5:45 (NASB)

Let's Get Started!

If you would like even more mojo for your tool belt, please visit http://silentbutsuperhero.com/ to receive even more valuable tools and free goodies as a thank-you for choosing my book. If you want to learn how I can help you implement these powerful concepts and tools in your own life, organization, or community, please email me at mindscope7@silentbutsuperhero.com. All fellow superheroes who purchased my book, don't forget to include the code "mindscope7" in your email, for free goodies and discounts on a variety of services, just for you! Just send an email with the subject line "I want to know," along with the above code, to receive details on the War Zone package.

I can't wait to work with you on building your own movement and watching the release of your own power and purpose for the betterment of humankind. Much love, strength, wisdom, and endurance upon your journey; we are here but for a short while. May this book serve as a guide toward the release of your own superpowers, then lead you toward the divinely specific, and purposeful, life that God had in mind when He first imagined your creation.

> There comes such a time in our lives when the decisiveness between courageous or cowardly actions becomes so critical that the entirety of humankind suffers a threat.
>
> —MindScope Seven

Hard-Line Rules

- To move beyond perceived and real boundaries, requires an authentic and intimate connection to divine power, indisputable of mortal man.
- Discovering your untapped power within, and then connecting it to purpose, can only be achieved by plugging into the correct source of a Higher Power and principles. Any human, male or female, can obtain limited power and purpose, but the one who plugs in correctly is only limited by his or her own efforts and obedience in His purpose.
- Remain authentic to your unique and specific design, in all that you do; however, does not negate the need or requirement to connect with a Higher Power.
- There is no pain-free or debt-free path; the key is to choose a predetermined price that you can afford. You must then accept and pay this price, for if not, you will pay far more than you ever imagined.

- Anyone who tells you that there is an easier or no-cost path is a determined liar, or truly ignorant and lacking correct understanding.
- You must keep your hands clean in all your dealings.
- Until your love for others is greater than your love for self, you will not be able to cross the "dangerous mine-covered fields of change"!
- Always think in terms of "this" or "that" when choosing. It is never "this" *and* "that."
- You must get your enemies to show their hands as completely as possible, while simultaneously ensuring that they remain unaware of your attention to them. Hold your own hand close and tight, only showing what you need. The opposition should never sense your intention of discovery; instead, quietly maneuver, unnoticed. This requires you to remain patient and to eat the punches thrown at you. This cannot be done in a state of pride, emotions, or selfish motives. You will get beat up nicely in this strategy! Plan for the eating of punches and stay focused only on the target of destination. Attitude adjustment is necessary to pull this off. It will strip you bare. It will force you to look weak and/or ignorant when in the active phase. Take no emotions or ego into this place. If you do, your movement will not succeed.
- Choose battles carefully; let most pass, and choose to lose others. You must keep your focus on the larger battle (big picture), or you will risk losing the war.
- Be keenly aware of the deep-rooted problem, or your efforts will be fruitless, dangerous, and even damaging to you and those you serve.
- You must become more than that of the enemy, stripping away your own weaknesses to the very best of your ability. Keep a constant eye on your goal and know that you are walking the narrow line required for victory.

- You must have skin in the game. If you are not feeling the pain of adjustment or sacrifice, you are *not* putting skin in the game. It *must* pose difficulty and require a process of giving up something as a personal sacrifice to the cause. The mere striking of a check is not good enough. This is a process of your own superpowers at work for purpose, for the cause. This is something unique to your talents or abilities, that only you can provide, making it critically necessary for us all to put skin in the game of change.

ABOUT THE AUTHOR

MINDSCOPE SEVEN has more than twenty-seven years of business experience, which included sales management and business ownership. Her paradoxical style goes against the expected, to render results in the most complicated, even dangerous, situations. Her strong perception of human behavior, combined with her humble beginnings, forced her to invent ways of overcoming disadvantaged positions. She learned to use disadvantage as the advantage. At the heart of her philosophies is the ability to understand and interpret the needs of the individuals she serves, and then to deliver purposeful, effective solutions to address those needs. Her no-nonsense, paradoxical style takes creativity to new levels for generating results and needed change. Her philosophies have been applied and proved successful in a variety of personal and business situations. MINDSCOPE SEVEN holds a unique position of tested theories that have been demonstrative for the entirety of her life—and that show how we all hold responsibility to one another in terms of connecting our God-given abilities to the common needs of humankind.

Through her own journey, she came to understanding that her unique set of skills and abilities were given to her for the very purpose of serving her fellow humans, oftentimes, against institutional flaws that worked against them. Her desire to find ethical, effective, people-oriented solutions led her to unusual approaches, which yielded results that others were not willing or able to match. Her spiritual foundation has always been the cornerstone of her philosophies and processes, guiding her often-unusual approach and strong desire to serve humankind.

MINDSCOPE SEVEN has successfully raised two children, along with the pressures of business ownership, and now feels her calling of service to be alleviating the suffering of her fellow humans and helping to effect the urgent changes needed for a more hopeful future, for our children and the generations to come.

A portion of all book sales will be donated to charities committed to the works of good stewardship.

Printed in the United States
By Bookmasters